Kumar Bhattacharyya: The Unsung Guru

Kumar Bhattacharyya

The Unsung Guru

Andrew Lorenz

RANDOM HOUSE
BUSINESS BOOKS

For Helen, James and Harry

Published by Business Books in 2002

1 3 5 7 9 10 8 6 4 2

Copyright © 2002 by Andrew Lorenz

Andrew Lorenz has asserted his right under the Copyright, Designs
and Patents Act 1988 to be identified as the author of this work

First published by Business Books in 2002.

Business Books
Random House, 20 Vauxhall Bridge Road,
London SW1V 2SA

Random House Australia (Pty) Limited
20 Alfred Street, Milsons Point, Sydney,
New South Wales 2061, Australia

Random House New Zealand Limited
18 Poland Road, Glenfield,
Auckland 10, New Zealand

Random House (Pty) Limited
Endulini, 5A Jubilee Road, Parktown 2193, South Africa

The Random House Group Limited Reg. No. 954009

www.randomhouse.co.uk

Papers used by Random House are natural,
recyclable products made from wood grown in sustainable forests;
the manufacturing processes conform to the environmental
regulations of the country of origin

ISBN 0 7126 7244 3

Typeset by Deltatype Ltd, Birkenhead, Merseyside

Printed and bound in Great Britain by
Mackays of Chatham plc, Kent

Introduction

When I was growing up in India, engineering was the driving force behind the development of India as a newly independent nation. Engineering had a massive status; there was a huge job of work to be done in creating the infrastructure of a modern country and to be an engineer was to be a key ingredient in that process.

India had created a new class of institution, the Indian Institutes of Technology (IIT's) to produce the required skills, and was turning out some very good engineers. As a student in the first one of these IIT's, at Kharagpur, I learnt a great deal. The curriculum was broad, I learnt humanities and sciences; being an engineer was respected and you knew that the broad range of skills you developed would be utilised.

I completed my education in engineering with a graduate apprenticeship with Lucas Industries, at that time a world leader in electrical engineering, before going on to Birmingham University to complete my MSc and PhD. I quickly realised that the vibrancy that existed for engineering in India, which I had expected to find in Britain, was not there. The passion had gone out of it.

The processes both in the way in which products were created and manufactured and the way companies were run, looked tired. I thought that I'd left the caste system behind in India, but the rigid hierarchy and narrowness of organisation, was replicated inside the British firms I encountered. Despite the fact that I was being trained inside one of the best engineering companies in Britain, when I looked around I could see that the outlook was poor.

As we moved from the swinging Sixties into the Seventies, manufacturing industry in Britain was hit by a double whammy: the sector did not have the intellectual horsepower to modernise itself and young people of the Beatles generation found the image of manufacturing a total turn off.

When I went to meetings with managers and directors from the leading Midlands manufacturing companies, they did not believe that the re-emerging Germany or Japan (especially not Japan) would be able to steal their imperial or commonwealth markets. As the wind of change was blowing through them, however, they were fast disappearing. Meanwhile the home market was facing intense competition from the same sources.

I had moved to Birmingham University on a Lucas Fellowship, thanks to Bert Everts, Group Manufacturing Director, who was a great support. I began to study manufacturing much more seriously in Germany, Japan and the USA and I could see immediately that there was a tremendous buzz in their engineering industries. When I saw the huge investment they were making in new technology and new products and the quality of the people that were coming out of their education systems, I began to realise the enormity of the challenge we were facing in this country. The gap was wide and getting wider.

The United States in particular had invested substantially in research into new materials and digital technologies funded largely by the defence and space agencies. The expansion in computer and simulation technology revolutionised the product development process, which lead to an exponential increase in product reliability. The Japanese onslaught came as a result of their training by the US after the war: they then put into practise what they had learnt. The Japanese produced well-designed, highly reliable, products at affordable prices. Their invasion of white goods and consumer electronics markets all but wiped out the European and US industry. Clearly they had some advantages as the cost of investment was low but their processes were based upon rigour in the product design process, disciplined manufacture with tremendous attention to detail from a well integrated supply chain.

Being based at Birmingham University, I was supervising many student projects at the huge British Leyland plant at Longbridge. It was obvious to me that the way the managers and workers were carrying on meant that they were committing suicide.

There was a total lack of quality manpower. The senior managers in many of the leading Midlands manufacturing companies that I'd met, looked provincial and positively unworldly in comparison with their international counterparts. When I told them what I'd seen in Germany and Japan, they either refused to believe or failed to appreciate what I was telling them. Many managers were appointed on their ability to manage their company's relationship with the trade unions, the principle requirement for which seemed to be their capacity to shout at and bully people. Industrial relations were a major problem, mainly due to the poor quality of management. The culture of manufacturing meant that most firms did not know how to use the best brains even when they had them.

During this time, although I was working in a university under the wonderful Professor Norman Dudley, we were unable to recruit the quality of students manufacturing really needed. Students were assessed by the papers they published, rather than by their application of engineering in the market place, which was somehow deemed grubby by academia. From the university's perspective, manufacturing was not only unfashionable, but as a subject was seen as a 'near-market' activity, which did not belong in a university environment.

Whilst in Germany, I'd visited many of the Technische Hochschule institutions which were established as a result of the educational policy debates held in the Sixties. The need to help German industry maintain its competitiveness in the international field, led to an increasing demand for better qualified personnel with the capacity to solve practical tasks quickly and successfully. This demand created the need for the Technische Hochschule and I felt that this was a model we could emulate. There was a clear demand in industry for better quality, brighter people. However, persuading the university that that demand could be met by designing a programme that would satisfy industry's requirements, was another matter altogether. I took my plan to the university, but they said that manufacturing was 'not the sort of thing' they should be doing. What had happened to the notion of scholarship?

I was still thinking about these ideas whilst putting together a range of automotive and aerospace firms into clubs involving assemblers and their suppliers. Clearly the firms were interested in this approach and I had floated my ideas with Dr Peter Davies of the Science and Engineering Research Council (SERC). He then took them to his Chairman, Professor (later Sir) Geoffrey Alan and we met and discussed my ideas.

Whilst these discussions were taking place, Monty Finniston had been touring the country preparing his report on engineering education. The problem I was trying to tackle was becoming a national issue. It was obvious that we had all reached the same conclusion, but what could we do about it?

My idea was to ignore academic snobbery, and, using the German model as a starting point, develop new learning pro-grammes to fill the gap, partly funded by resources from SERC. At that time most postgraduate places were going to overseas students and there was little that was appropriate for the main engineering manufacturing businesses. The dual objective was a programme that would act as a retention tool for the brightest graduate recruits whilst training existing managers to utilise the skills of these young graduates.

Out of those conversations an initial group of five firms agreed to support the programme; British Leyland, Lucas, GKN, Shorts and Rolls Royce Aerospace. Not long afterwards they were joined by British Airways and British Aerospace. Whilst many firms did not feel able to work with universities or feel able to utilise the bright young people they turned out, I did have my supporters in industry, without whom my ideas would never have reached fruition. People like Bill Horton at BL, Frank Turner and Phil Ruffles at Rolls Royce, Roy McNulty and Brian Carlin at Shorts and Alistair Cumming at BA helped me make the programme a reality.

It was just prior to this that Jack Butterworth approached me, he was then the Vice-Chancellor of the University of Warwick, a very small new university. He saw I had a good idea with some serious backers and offered a green field site in a new institution, which had few barriers to development. It was a good location, close to the centre of the UK's manufacturing base and I was able to take the Chair in Manufacturing that Warwick had established to enable me to become the first Professor to deal with manufacturing as a whole in the UK.

When I came to Warwick University in 1980, to start WMG, the signs for manufacturing in the UK were not good. When I travelled around the world the image of manufacturing and of Britain was poor. Manufacturing was in crisis and Universities were facing the first round of cutbacks. There could not be a more inauspicious time to begin a new institution. My idea was essentially a very simple one: if manufacturing was to survive and prosper in the intensely competitive global market place we needed to harness the intellectual horsepower of our brightest and best young graduates. This was my attempt to create a mechanism to channel bright young engineers into British manufacturing industry.

This turned out to be a wonderful relationship; Warwick

provided a super environment, in which, what became known as the Warwick Manufacturing Group could prosper and grow. The Group in turn, with its substantial relationships with industry enabled Warwick to punch above its weight. I owe a debt of gratitude to Jack Butterworth and Geoffrey Alan who took a gamble on me when many of the engineering institutions were sceptical. I hope what has been achieved since shows their trust was not misplaced.

Since then, of course, WMG has expanded into research activities, other sectors of industry and even other countries. Since I set out on this journey, many have joined me on the road. What I have been doing over the past twenty odd years now looks like common-sense, but at the time there was a huge culture gap between industry and universities. It was hard work building that first bridge and I hope the story of the Warwick Manufacturing Group encourages others help us to continue the process.

Britain's economy has changed beyond recognition over the last twenty years; we in Britain today have the best regulatory and fiscal framework in Europe. Manufacturing as a percentage of GDP has fallen, as has been the case in other industrialised nations. British industry has been good at restructuring existing operations, outsourcing and taking advantage of business opportunities. Large amounts of outsourcing may explain some of the anomalies in the statistics regarding GDP. The companies with excellent product bases are few and far between and that makes long-term sustainability of the manufacturing sector vulnerable. This is due to are poor record of industrial R&D and innovation. Whilst Britain has changed enormously, our competitors have also changed and furthermore there has been an unprecedented rate at which the manufacturing industries have grown in the emerging economies such as China, India and Eastern Europe. All manufacturing industries in order to be competitive have to be knowledge-based. And since there is an abundance of good quality manpower in emerging markets coupled with liberalisation taking place throughout the world there is an unprecedented demand for manufactured goods in emerging economies. So the perception that emerging economies are not likely to be knowledge-based is a myth. And hence industry in Britain, in order to maintain and improve its competitive position must as a priority improve its ability to develop products.

Everything we do is engineered and if we can capture the imagination of youngsters and excite them by modernising the way we teach and attract them, thereby unleashing their innovative power on manufacturing industry, well I think we can win.

Kumar Bhattacharyya, 2002

Contents

Chapter One

Bridging The Gap

The Prime Minister took his seat at the small table. On either side of Tony Blair sat Stephen Alambritis, head of Britain's National Federation of Small Businesses; and the Premier's host for the afternoon, Kumar Bhattacharyya, founder and chairman of WMG, Warwick Manufacturing Group.

Grouped around this trio, tightly packed on tiered seats in the restricted space, sat 150 invited guests from the West Midlands business community. Representatives of the regional Confederation of British Industry and Chambers of Commerce sat cheek by compressed jowl with senior executives such as Mike Beasley, Jaguar's manufacturing director, and local entrepreneurs. Crammed in behind them on one side of the makeshift auditorium was a small army of media men, reporters and photographers.

Two days earlier, Blair had visited Buckingham Palace to ask the Queen to dissolve Parliament and call a General Election for 7 June 2001. He was now barely a month from making history as the first

Labour prime minister to be re-elected with a majority large enough to guarantee a full second term of government.

For a Labour leader who prided himself on having reformed the party's historic hostility to the agents of wealth creation, today's event would strike a keynote for the forthcoming campaign. As Blair's first election interface with industrialists, it would provide him with a platform to assert his claims that Labour now appreciated the importance of British business.

Appropriately, considering that he was visiting an organisation dedicated to breaking down the barriers between industry and academia, one of Blair's themes was partnership: in his case, partnership between politics and business. 'Always the most dangerous thing in our country was when one political party was with business and the other wasn't. Whoever is in power should be pro-business,' he said. 'There will be times when we have disagreements. But as far as my own party is concerned, the partnership with business is better than it has ever been.'

His apparently assured success at the ballot box, as forecast by every opinion poll, helped to explain Blair's quiet confidence and relaxed mood. So did the fact that he was in familiar surroundings. Less than six months earlier, he had chosen the Warwick University campus, home to WMG, as the venue for his public farewell to Bill Clinton, in several respects his political mentor, who was then nearing the end of his second presidential term. It was thanks to Bhattacharyya's work over the last twenty years which had raised the profile of Warwick University and thus secured for Warwick the honour of ringing down the curtain in Britain on the two men's special relationship.

The relationship between Bhattacharyya and the Blair government was, in the very British context of generally fraught university attitudes to politics, equally special. It was the product of elements on both the political and the academic side. From New Labour, during its evolution through the 1990s, there was a desire to achieve legitimacy and credibility with opinion-makers and policy-formers in all walks of economic life. That, however, did not explain why, of all people in all universities, the New Labour focus should fall so strongly on the founder-director of Warwick Manufacturing Group.

The answer went to the heart of Bhattacharyya's achievement and the place that he had carved out, over two decades, in the nexus between government, industry and academia. For most people active in the higher education system, this area was either a no-go area or a no-man's land. For the scion of a highly respected in both business and politics, Brahmin family, it was a fertile, stimulating interface — a *raison d'être*.

Three features distinguished Bhattacharyya's achievement: his mastery of the discipline of engineering; his internationalism; and his determination to bridge the great and historic divide between academia and business. Bhattacharyya himself was the embodiment of that refusal to accept enclosure in a single world.

His work appeared to make him an entrepreneurial academic, but he bridled at the description. In heart and mind, he was an academic entrepreneur. But here, too, he defied easy characterisation. Bhattacharyya was not the kind of university-derived entrepreneur who had become a commonplace in Britain during the two decades of WMG's existence. He did not belong to that group of professors and postgraduates, notably in Cambridge's Silicon Fen, who had spun companies off their areas of expertise and headed for the international stock markets. The centre of his gravity lay uniquely elsewhere.

His political dimension was also fundamentally different from the conventional politics of university or business life. Certainly, Bhattacharyya knew all about those "small" politics: his first attempt to establish a manufacturing group, at Birmingham University in the late 1970s, foundered on academic envy, intrigue and, almost certainly, the crude prejudice of an establishment against an outsider.

The politics that drew Bhattacharyya, and which were drawn to

3

him, were those of national government. His ability to exert a certain influence in the state's affairs, or at least to exercise a voice to which the nation's top ministers and mandarins paid some attention, derived from two elements: his independence, and the singular vision that imbued his work.

The respect in which he was held by two contrasting administrations – those of Margaret Thatcher and Tony Blair, both of whom he advised on matters industrial, technological and educational – testified to the power of that vision and his ability to translate it into an academically and commercially successful entity. Both Thatcher and Blair were radicals: she a revolutionary in Tory guise; he a social democrat in, initially, the most hidebound party in Britain. They shaped their governments in their respective images. Bhattacharyya, the academic who had slaughtered the sacred cows in technology management education, was a natural point of reference for both of them.

His independent means, the fact that he owed nothing to anyone, exerted a powerful fascination for many of their supporters, but also provided a constant reassurance. Bhattacharyya could always be relied on for dispassionate, objective, well-informed and, above all, disinterested advice. That kind of entirely untainted expertise was worth its weight in gold – particularly for Thatcher, as she set about uprooting the post-war consensus that had led Britain down the primrose path to near-disaster.

Bhattacharyya certainly enjoyed the "buzz" of tackling complex problems at the fuzzy interface of business, politics and international affairs. And while he is fairly shy, he is never fazed and always at ease with the most senior figures from business and politics from around the world. Most satisfying for him, though, was the endorsement, sometimes explicit, more often implicit, that this respect conferred on his pioneering approach to the business of management education. Above all, his natural gratification at being admitted to the inner counsels of industrial policy never gave way to self-satisfaction and the complacency that dulls performance. A restless mind in a restless body, he remained alert to the shifts in the tectonic plates of world management thought, constantly seeking to remain at the cutting edge while piling up the air miles between WMG and the points on his global compass.

Wherever he went, Bhattacharyya never forgot the essential need to remain relevant to his customers, be they companies or individual students. At no time did he close his eyes to innovation; he was always ready to embrace anything that made sense to him and that would refresh the content of his programmes. But here, too, he defied danger. WMG was constantly evolving, but it never descended into trendiness or faddism. The group in 2002 had taken many turnings and made many new departures since its creation twenty-two years earlier, yet a consistency of principle and purpose permeated its culture of responsiveness and accountability.

Despite the team of strong and experienced characters that Bhattacharyya had assembled through the years, WMG's culture and modus operandi were moulded in the image of its founding father. And he, appropriately enough, attributed his corpus of strong precepts to his own father. 'As a boy, I always wanted to go beyond the norm,' Bhattacharyya said. 'That came from my father. My value systems were all fundamentally given to me by him.'

Bhattacharyya senior won a series of gold medals – awards for academic achievement – as an undergraduate in an India still governed by the British Empire. He visited Britain before the Second World War, and went on to become an academic at the Indian Institute of Science. His son, born on 6 June 1940 and growing up in the immediate post-Independence era, demonstrated an aptitude for engineering in his early teens by building a whole car from scratch 'for the hell of it'.

These were high days for engineering in India. 'There was huge growth in engineering; everybody wanted to be an engineer,' Bhattacharyya recalled. Amid intense competition for places, he gained entrance to the Indian Institute of Technology, where he took a degree in mechanical engineering. His ambitions, however, extended beyond the conventional confines of such an education.

'I didn't want to be a run-of-the-mill academic or engineer,' he said. 'Business is what has always given me the buzz. I have a pretty low boredom threshold, so I have always needed the adrenalin to flow as much as possible.'

Bhattacharyya therefore had a quest for new challenges in mind when, aged twenty, he followed a well-worn path for Indian technical graduates – to serve an apprenticeship in Britain at a well-regarded engineering company. His employer-teacher was Lucas CAV, the diesel engine components subsidiary of Lucas Industries, a blue-chip pillar of the British engineering establishment which had been founded in 1862 by Joseph Lucas in Great King Street, Birmingham, to make bicycle lamps.

Unlike most of his compatriots, who served their apprenticeship in Britain and then returned home, Bhattacharyya decided to stay on. 'It was expected that I would go abroad and get trained. It was not expected that I would stay,' he said. 'It was difficult for my family when I decided to stay. India was growing and there was pressure from everywhere for me to come home. I came from a very orthodox Brahmin caste. There were questions – had I opted out?'

The reverse was true: Bhattacharyya had opted into the first radical move in his unorthodox career. He had a very specific reason for remaining at Lucas: 'I wanted to learn how a big company works,' he said. He also, he said, 'got a buzz from being in an alien environment. I was the only Indian at Lucas at the time. When I walked around the factory floor, people stared at me.' In the process, he learned an important lesson: that successful management requires winning the confidence of colleagues. 'The art of doing things is to ensure you make the other person comfortable. It is when people see you as a competitor that they start looking at you differently and uncooperatively.'

Bhattacharyya put his extended Lucas apprenticeship to good use. He stayed six years, and visited many firms in the Lucas supply and customer chain. Lucas also sent him to the University of

6

Birmingham to take a master's degree in engineering. Before he had completed his PhD, he was appointed lecturer at Birmingham and, with Lucas' support, began the process of establishing a manufacturing centre within the university. Drawing on his family's range of international contacts, he travelled widely in the ensuing years studying and gaining experience of manufacturing in Germany, Japan and the United States. In Japan, for example, he was able to study, long before it became generally known and revered as the template for lean manufacturing, the Toyota production system. What he saw in Nagoya, Toyota's manufacturing base, made an indelible impression and created a lasting influence on his approach to both technology management and development.

Bhattacharyya did not remain in Asia. In 1979, armed with the perspective and the knowledge he had gained since his Lucas apprenticeship, he returned to his industrial alma mater in Birmingham. At first sight, it seemed a strange relocation. The swinging, confident Britain of the World Cup year of 1966 had faded into a deeply troubled nation in such economic decline that it had become a commonplace to brand it the sick man of Europe.

A minority Labour government led by Jim Callaghan had spent the second half of the decade on a political life-support machine – the Lib–Lab pact, under which the Liberals kept their crucial handful of MPs behind Labour. Callaghan was finally defeated in the May 1979 general election by the largely unknown, and certainly untried, Margaret Thatcher.

Thatcher inherited a country whose competitiveness had been undermined in vast tracts of industry by open war between weak managements and overmighty unions, with the divisions in union ranks between full-time officials and shop stewards contributing at times to a state of near-anarchy. Prerequisites for competitiveness, such as continuous production, fault-free products and adequate returns on investment, were quite unattainable. Industry was a stop-start zone where production was frequently interrupted by strikes, wildcat and official. The sight of any new piece of capital equipment was enough to prompt union demands for higher pay, thereby negating the purpose of investing in the equipment and nullifying the potential for enhancing competitiveness.

Management, beaten down by more than a decade of union militancy, was indecisive and defeatist. Its morale was at rock bottom. Its quality was poor – no one in their right senses wanted a job in the losing battleground that was manufacturing industry. The British tradition of the gifted amateur persisted among the engineers who ran companies, except for the fact that many of the amateurs could not be called gifted. And in any case, many companies were run not by engineers but by accountants who knew the price of every bit of technology but the value of none of it.

A less fertile ground for Bhattacharyya's ambitions seemed hard to imagine. But, like a true entrepreneur, he spotted opportunity amid the chaos. Britain, as ever quick to debate the causes of its decline – even if it was painfully slow to tackle those factors – had embarked on a new round of self-analysis. In the engineering profession, this bout of navel-gazing had led to the appointment of Sir Monty Finniston, former chairman of the state-owned British Steel Corporation (BSC), to conduct an inquiry into the methods by which Britain educated and trained its engineers.

The Finniston Report, when it emerged the following year, contained more substance than many such inquiries, before or since. This was largely due to the mettle of its chairman: Finniston had been removed from the chair at BSC by Callaghan's Labour government in 1976, after telling ministers that the company needed to axe 20,000 jobs from its 220,000-strong workforce in the short term. In the long term, said Finniston, BSC would need only 50,000 employees if it were to become internationally competitive. This was a prophetic message, but it was also unpalatable to a government many of whose most senior ministers occupied constituencies in steel plant areas.

The combative Glaswegian's days as a mover and shaker were not done, however. Engineering Our Future, the report his committee produced in 1980, dissected the shortcomings of both engineering education and the companies that employed those engineering graduates. It highlighted, for instance the preponderance of accountants, rather than engineers, on the boards of British companies – a situation that was to become even more pronounced during the recession that was about to strike, and which did not apply in any of Britain's leading competitor countries, including the United States, Germany, Japan and France.

At the heart of Engineering Our Future, Finniston identified a fundamental mismatch between the supplier and the customer – between engineering education and the needs of Britain's engineering and manufacturing industry. In general, Britain's universities, abetted by the professional engineering institutions, were turning out people with qualifications and skills that were unsuited to the requirements of UK plc.

The corollary was equally basic: what companies wanted from their engineering graduates – people with a grasp of management techniques and financial know-how, as well as contemporary technical expertise – they were not getting. 'If you took an engineering doctorate and put that person in a factory, the cleaner was more use to the company than the graduate engineer,' is how one of Bhattacharyya's staff sums up, with just a touch of caricature, the underlying theme of the Finniston report.

Engineering Our Future was still in the works when Bhattacharyya set foot on British soil again. But its subject matter was high on the industrial agenda. Lucas asked him to set up a course that would make 'manufacturing' a university subject. The natural home for such a project seemed to be the University of Birmingham, so A.E. (Bert) Everts, the Manufacturing Director of Joseph Lucas Ltd. persuaded the Lucas board to endow a chair there, for Bhattacharyya.

It was an unhappy experience, one which even today Bhattacharyya is reluctant to discuss in detail. Almost immediately, he encountered deep resentment of what he was trying to do, resentment that was both professional – a classic case of academic envy – and, it seems most likely, personal and racial. In no time at

9

all, unsubstantiated but poisonous stories about Bhattacharyya – about the nature of his independence, of his affiliations and so on – were being circulated in the city. Their wellspring was a classic collision between the ambitious, thrusting radical and the entrenched, reactionary establishment – and then, as now, few establishments are more reactionary than educational ones. The impact was fatal to Bhattacharyya's hopes of making Birmingham his base. But the real loser was the university. Its loss was its nearby rival's gain, and that gain was permanent.

'After Birmingham, I had offers from all over the world,' said Bhattacharyya. 'But Warwick came along and offered me a free rein.' For someone with Bhattacharyya's ideas and ambitions, such an offer was unrefusable. The man who made it was quite a character in his own right. Professor Jack Butterworth, vice-chancellor of the University of Warwick, was determined to establish his relatively young institution – Warwick was one of the new redbrick universities created in the 1960s to meet the explosion in demand for higher education – in the front rank of British universities. To do that, he needed both talent and differentiation. Bhattacharyya's concept of a postgraduate course in manufacturing management offered both: Butterworth immediately recognised both the capabilities of the man and the distinctiveness of his vision.

There was a particular appositeness in this conjunction of institution and individual. From its inception, Warwick had set as one of its main objectives the need for 'a close relationship with industry'. It had emphasised management studies and engineering courses and numerous companies were encouraged to endow chairs. As Martin J. Wiener remarked in his seminal study of Britain's industrial decline, *English Culture and the Decline of the Industrial Spirit*, 'the dream of a great Midlands MIT began to take shape'.

However, as Wiener noted: 'The dream blew up in 1970, caught between pressures from businessmen and an increasingly antibusiness student movement.' A student revolt ensued, with all the accoutrements familiar from the London School of Economics turmoil in the high days of '68. 'Students and faculty radicals struck a responsive chord in the educated public with their charges of commercial corruption of higher national values at Warwick,' remarked Wiener. He quoted a passage from *Warwick University Ltd*, an anti-industry treatise by the Warwick rebels, both students and academics.

> It is sobering to realise that the mid-Atlantic of Midlands Motor and Aircraft Industry [the local industrial community] offers one possible model of a British future. It is a . . . brash, amoral, pushful world of expense-account living, lavish salesmanship, cocktail bars in restored sixteenth-century inglenooks, and of refined managerial techniques of measured day-work; a world of mergers and takeovers, of the unregenerate, uninhibited Mammon of the Sunday business supplements.

All that was missing was a reference to dark Satanic mills.

The 1970 reaction brought Warwick's first industrial partnership experiment to a halt. As a metaphor for Britain's macro-industrial convulsions, it would be hard to beat. In an uncanny sense, it presaged the U-turn by Ted Heath's Tory government, which was elected in the year of the Warwick troubles on a manifesto that promised to reverse Britain's economic decline by allowing market forces free rein. Those intentions were destroyed by the emergence of lame ducks – Rolls-Royce in 1971 and Govan Shipbuilders the same year – that Heath agreed to rescue. Then came the miners' strikes and the final disappearance of the promised Heath revolution.

Just as Thatcher's election in 1979 signified a second attempt to reverse Britain's post-war decline by strict adherence to free market economics, so Butterworth's new Warwick was picking up the unravelled threads of the academia–industry alliance. There was a Warwick Business School; soon, there was a centre for the study of small business development headed by Dr David Storey, who was lured from the pioneering Centre for Urban and Regional Development Studies at the University of Newcastle.

But the opportunity embodied by Bhattacharyya was something else again. Apart from his expertise in manufacturing technology, the Professor came with an assiduously developed range of contacts in automotive and aerospace companies at home and overseas – Warwick's natural constituency because of the large local representation of these businesses. Long before the term 'cluster' became an economic development cliché, the Midlands was home to large-scale clusters of auto and aero manufacturers.

More compelling even than his know-how and his contacts book was Bhattacharyya's philosophy, which accorded perfectly with Butterworth's own outlook and with the heritage of the university. Bhattacharyya said: 'In the seventies, the divide between academia and industry was huge. I thought, "Let me fill that gap and show that it can be done." We had wonderful brainpower in universities and we were getting fresh blood here all the time. But manufacturing didn't get the quality of people that it needed. I identified that the major requirement was good feedstock to help companies develop the technology base that could help the UK have world-class businesses.'

Bhattacharyya's benchmarking was international. 'I looked at industry here and compared it with the huge changes that were taking place internationally. That gave me the perception that the quality of investment, the type of people that we had in Britain and the regulatory framework would never allow the UK to compete.'

He anticipated the difficulty, in this environment, of winning acceptance for his approach. The Finniston report provided corroboration and justification, and the Thatcher government removed the alibis for poor industrial management: 'Government intervention was like opium – it had created life support systems so that nobody wanted to survive by themselves. You were dealing with a management style and mentality that had been formed over 30 years – to some extent, we were not so different from the Soviet Union, where everything was dependent on the state.'

Suddenly, managers had to work out the answers and take decisions for themselves. They needed guidance; they needed education. 'The product base, our national manufacturing asset, was inadequate. To improve it required a vastly-better quality of decision-making,' Bhattacharyya said. 'In the whole area of design for manufacturing products and processes, for instance, Britain had been falling ever further behind its competitors for decades.' The country had a long history of failure to commercialise innovation successfully. Imaginative products frequently collapsed in the market – or failed to reach it – because companies could not make them reliable or sell them at prices that were both competitive and sufficiently profitable to sustain the business.

To Bhattacharyya, the gulf between conception and realisation flowed directly from the lack of top-class engineering managers. 'From top to bottom in industry, there was no intellect. We lacked rigour; we lacked structure. That was a reflection of the education system and the way people got trained. There was no realisation that, in the world outside, there was intellect and capability that we simply did not have. It wasn't much to do with investors or the City. The record of graduates going into industry was alarming, and nobody seemed to do anything about it.'

He had no illusions about the size of the mountain he was setting out to conquer: the historic bias, rooted deep in British culture and society, against engineering and manufacturing. Throughout the world, 'engineer' was a title that commanded respect, a profession to rank alongside doctor, lawyer, teacher. There was only one developed economy where the engineer did not enjoy this kind of respect: Britain, where the term was associated with people (invariably men) in blue overalls who came to mend the washing machine or the boiler. In the UK, engineer was a dirty word.

Wiener quotes a story dating from the mid-1970s about one engineer, who was taken by his father, a bank manager, to lunch at his club. Before they went in, the father said: 'I don't know how the members will regard an engineer.'

To borrow the famous Groucho Marx line, engineers did not want to be in any club that would have them as a member. They wanted recognition and appreciation from the establishment that valued the other professions: medicine, law, even accountancy. Instead, they found themselves caught in a vicious circle. Their professional education was narrow and theoretical rather than practical. More often than not, because of their lack of appropriate management and financial education, they were also-rans in boardroom pecking orders. There were few exceptions to this unhappy rule. One of the few was Sir Francis, later Lord, Tombs, an engineer who recognised the shortcomings of his professional education and put himself through night school accountancy training so that he could compete for the highest corporate roles. Tombs became chairman of a string of famous engineering companies, including Rolls-Royce.

The problem, by the late 1970s, had moved on from that identified by the author C.P. Snow when he wrote in the sixties of the schism in British political, academic and economic life between the artists and the scientists, the gentlemen and the players, the amateurs and the professionals. Snow criticised the ingrained British hostility to science, applying as a test for all members of the governing class whether any knew the Second Law of Thermodynamics.

The great divide that Bhattacharyya recognised was different: between those who knew the Second Law and those who could use it to develop innovative products or processes. Bhattacharyya's contrast was between the theoretical and the practical, the academic and the commercial, the pure and the applied. 'Manufacturing wasn't respectable,' he said. 'People thought that it wasn't rigorous enough. This was not the case in the United States — at

MIT or Stanford. But here, technologists and engineers were always seen as second-rate citizens. Science took precedence. Here in Britain, you weren't kosher unless you were a scientist or a pure engineer. This concept was crazy – like a medical school without patients. It was like approaching manufacturing in a vacuum, producing papers all about the past.'

It was the difference between a very British value set and a technocratic skill set, and it marked Britain out not only from the US, but from the rest of Europe. In France, managers, civil servants and engineers shared a homogeneous education in the Grandes Écoles and were almost interchangeable, moving fluidly out of one world into another and back again. In Italy, captains of industry were distinguished by the title 'Engineer'; in West Germany, as one commentator quoted by Wiener observed in 1976: 'The ideas that industry is not a fitting occupation of a gentleman (old version) or for an intellectual (new version) seem not to have existed. Neither making money nor making three-dimensional artefacts are culturally dubious activities.'

Given his background, Bhattacharyya carried none of the conventional British baggage about manufacturing industry. But there was more to his approach than merely the individualism of a gifted outsider free from a cultural mindset. When Bhattacharyya surveyed the divide between the academic and commercial worlds, he exposed Britain's fundamental competitive weakness: its persistent failure to convert undoubted intellectual horsepower into hard commercial realities that the customer, be it company or consumer, wanted to buy. He turned a spotlight on the country's sustained inability either to transfer innovative technologies into world-beating products, or, just as frequent, to manage the successful development of innately world-leading products.

The defining characteristics of Bhattacharyya's approach flowed from these principles. One was his flexibility. Instead of treating engineering business management, the subject of his teaching programmes, as a collection of prescriptive tablets of stone, to be handed down *ex cathedra* by the institution to the student, he emphasised a responsive approach to the corporate client.

This 'listening' ethic differentiated him from both the British academic traditionalists with their rigid textbooks and powerful heritage, and the great American management institutions, which presented their customers, both individual students and corporations, with a set of lessons that they were invited to take or leave. Established institutions such as Imperial College and Cambridge University, MIT and Harvard Business School could, of course, afford such an approach. Their names and those of their alumni preceded them. Their brands drew strength from that continuity.

Bhattacharyya was in a very different position. The unit he formed in Warwick's engineering department was a start-up enterprise whose brand he had to build from scratch. In such circumstances, he had to find a different way into the hearts and minds of his clientele. But it is doubtful, even if his Manufacturing Group had been founded in a more conventional environment, that his approach would have been any different. His combination of intellectual knowledge and commercial flair told him that the customer-driven approach must be correct. It was neither a corruption of some academic ideal, nor a bastardised form of management training: it was the best and most logical means available to achieve his goal of commercially relevant education and applied research.

There was a clear equation between Bhattacharyya's customer-led approach and the Japanese manufacturing doctrine that swept over Western companies in the 1980s like a Hokusai tidal wave. The historic theory of production push, which dated back to Henry Ford's assembly line, was eclipsed by the concept of market pull. Its manifestation in manufacturing practice was the break-up of the Fordian unitary production line into production cells, attended by such features as team working to devolve decision-making, just-in-time lineside component delivery to minimise inventory, and total preventative maintenance to achieve maximum availability of expensive machinery. Mass production was superseded by lean manufacturing, opening the way, years later, to the concept of mass customisation. Bhattacharyya did not, of course, invent the concept of lean manufacturing. But, informed by his knowledge of Toyota, he imported it into Britain. Under his aegis, cellular manufacturing was fully realised in Britain for the first time at British Leyland's (BL's) Cowley, Oxford factory, replete with mini-managing directors running their own workforce teams.

For Bhattacharyya, however, there was much more to manufacturing than, literally, manufacturing. The philosophical cornerstone of his approach was simple but radical: technology alone was not enough. Technological sophistication was, of course, an important sine qua non of economic success, but it was neither an end in itself nor a guarantor of growth. Like an industrial process, technology was the – advanced – raw material which had to be manufactured into an end-product by well-educated men and women schooled in the gamut of industrial management skills.

Bhattacharyya was, as the England football manager Sir Alf Ramsey once remarked of his World Cup-winning midfielder Martin Peters, years ahead of his time. Again, the influence on his thinking of his experience with Toyota could be discerned. But while he admired and adapted the car-maker's infinite attention to detail and the extraordinary rigour of its manufacturing techniques, Bhattacharyya never settled for the Japanese doctrine of aiming to be an outstanding second rather than an indifferent first. He believed passionately in innovation, in the potential to be an outstanding first. To him this was the ultimate goal, the way to harness German and Japanese manufacturing discipline to British flair and creativity.

Four of Bhattacharyya's key staff – Gordon Brace, Michael James-Moore, Trevor Broughton and Vinesh Raja – summarised the four pillars of this philosophy in a 1999 lecture subtitled 'Innovation Needs People'.

Technology does not automatically yield innovation; imagination and marketing skills are also required. Technology cannot be contained in a machine or a piece of software. It has an element of motivation and personal know-how. Successful transfer takes time and human contact, and that contact must be mutually supportive. The successful inventors and developers of technological processes are likely to be mobile. Organisations must build this supposition into their fabric and aim to husband their knowledge base in a Learning Organisation.

This was a holistic vision. Bhattacharyya saw a natural indivisibility between engineering business management and technology research and development. From the outset, he conceived of an interface between the two streams, each reinforcing the other. Traditionally, British universities had pursued both activities but in parallel, not criss-crossing lines. Bhattacharyya's motive force for emphasising the interface between the two was his conviction that, while technology was a prerequisite for competitive success, in isolation it was a recipe for sterility.

Only when technology was married with the human factor could it produce a living organism – a working product or process that could create a leading edge in the marketplace. 'In manufacturing, technology is a core competence,' Bhattacharyya said. 'But the reason why the Germans are so good at engineering is because they have the skill base to use their technology to make robust products. In Britain, we have the skill base at an upper level to do the blue-sky research, but we don't have the skill base that provides the rigour and the detail that launches a successful product. I was trying to bridge that gap.' That philosophical, cultural and practical pole was where he came from – and that, over more than two decades, is where he went.

Chapter Two

High Technology, High Politics

Jack Butterworth recognised a motivated man. He gave Kumar Bhattacharyya a title, Professor of Manufacturing Systems, a chair – the kind you physically sit on, rather than figuratively teach from – and a table. The furniture was in a two-room office on the second floor of the Department of Mechanical Engineering. To this day, Bhattacharyya works from the spacious inner room – now more lavishly equipped with a sofa and a large desk – while his secretary, Mary, and her assistant, Haseena, occupy the outer office. But Butterworth also gave Bhattacharyya something far more precious: a free hand, as far as the university statutes allowed, to build his enterprise.

Warwick's new recruit immediately established his first principle: to bridge the university–industry divide by a 'total commitment to partnership' between the two worlds. 'I said to myself, "Who are my customers?" They were not Joe Bloggs, who applies to any old university for a degree. They were the companies whose people I wanted to teach and whose technology I wanted to help develop. My starting point was straightforward: unless I developed a real partnership with these companies, I could not possibly know their needs.'

Later, the mission statement was refined into a kind of motto: 'Academic excellence with industrial relevance'. Bhattacharyya noted that few people except for him and his vice-chancellor believed the hybrid would succeed. 'There was an expectation that this experimental mixture of university and industry would be a failure. The differing interests of the two parties would mean that teaching and research programmes would be poorly focused and ultimately doomed.'

The Warwick Manufacturing Group, as Bhattacharyya and Butterworth named the new unit, opened for business on 1 October 1980. It was structured as an 'intermediate institute' – part of the university, organisationally as well as physically inside the Department of Engineering, but at liberty to become self-funding rather than dependent on government grants allocated through the university administrators. Not for the last time in WMG's history, this licence to self-generate funds reflected a happy union of principle and practicality. Bhattacharyya's entrepreneurial credo demanded such freedom, but, as it happened, WMG's inception coincided with the newly elected Thatcher government's squeeze on public spending, which led to extensive cutbacks across the further and higher education sectors.

Like many innovative start-ups, WMG did not enjoy a smooth path to growth. Bhattacharyya's first efforts to establish his technology development activity foundered on a lack of interest from his target market. The recession, triggered by the 1979 oil price shock that sent the petro-pound into orbit, burst upon manufacturers with such force that numerous firms failed and those that did not had to fight desperately for survival. Many caught a cold. ICI, the renowned bellwether of the British economy, suffered a profits meltdown and slashed its previously sacrosanct dividend. GKN, another industrial stalwart, slumped into loss, casting a pall over the whole engineering sector. As these giants sneezed and stumbled, many smaller firms were stricken with hypothermia. Investment was cut to the bone as companies struggled for life. Workforces that had become steadily more bloated in the inflation-ridden sixties and seventies were now decimated at a stroke. In such circumstances, few firms had the time, the money or the inclination to focus on modernising their technology base.

Ever-sensitive to the priorities of his customers, Bhattacharyya changed course. Instead of concentrating on new product development, he decided to emphasise the higher education activity of the new group and its focus on manufacturing process. Here he struck a chord. Companies did not have resources to spare and spend on R&D, but they most certainly did want to extract maximum benefit from the people that they retained. That required greater management quality, which in turn necessitated skills teaching. In the West Midlands, Bhattacharyya found a ready audience for WMG's graduate teaching programme. He developed a 'club', eventually comprising about thirty companies, who would send graduate recruits to Warwick for post-experience education in engineering and management. At the same time, Warwick staff were seconded to the companies so that they could help the graduates deploy their newly acquired skills in the real business environment.

One of the WMG mentors was Rajat Roy, an expert in the use of simulation to enhance design for manufacturing, who had worked with Bhattacharyya at Birmingham during the Professor's last two years there. In a way, Roy had been in at the birth of Bhattacharyya's new venture: he had come over to Warwick for a celebratory drink the night WMG opened for business. Nine months later, in June 1981, he formally joined the new group. At that time, it was a small team – no more than ten people. 'There were so few of us, everybody had to turn their hand to whatever needed doing,' Roy recalled.

Roy found his services required at BL, the state-controlled vehicles leviathan that dominated the West Midlands industrial scene. BL's Austin Rover cars group was in the throes of the most critical product launches in its recent history, the 'M' cars – Metro, Maestro and Montego. Although Metro, launched in 1980, had been an outstanding success, the company was struggling with Maestro and Montego. The problems had highlighted Austin Rover's desperate need to raise the quality of its middle and line management and to improve its manufacturing processes – and Roy was dispatched to Longbridge, where the Maestro was due to be produced, to help solve some of the manufacturing headaches.

'The Maestro line had been installed, but they were having some difficulty in meeting the pre-production volumes,' Roy said. 'That had an effect on quality, because if you are fire-fighting, quality suffers.' WMG's work did not save Maestro from being a disappointment in sales terms, but it at least enabled Austin Rover to improve the build quality of the vehicles. 'That gave us credibility in their eyes, and convinced them of the need for simulation before you make major investment decisions. From then on, we did a host of work for the company.'

Roy's project went hand-in-hand with teaching input by WMG into Austin Rover and some of its key suppliers, including Lucas Industries. Rolls-Royce, the aero-engine group, was also an early customer of WMG's post-graduate programme, thanks to Group Manufacturing Director Trevor Salt and then Bill Wood and Frank Turner. 'The teaching side started in mid-1981,' Roy said. 'It was a joint thing: the two activities, teaching and project work, had to go hand-in-hand. You don't really have credibility on the teaching side unless you can go out and do something with what you are talking about.'

Walking the walk was part of the WMG ethos from day one, and so was the partnership approach. Company staff were encouraged to lecture at WMG. 'Right from the start, it was not a case of us pushing our ideas,' Roy said. 'It was a partnership.

People in each of the customer companies were taking an active part in developing what was required. By and large, a number of people – some from WMG and others from the companies – sat down together to produce an outline of a particular module and then left it to a few individuals to flesh out that module. The technology modules came first; the business modules slightly later on.'

John Donne had the sonnet, Edward Lear the limerick. Bhattacharyya used the teaching module. With the module, he found the perfect form for translating his concept of work-related higher education into reality on the shop floor and in the lecture theatre.

Bhattacharyya did not invent the module system – by the time he set up WMG, it had been in use for many years, notably in the Open University. But he saw its potential to deliver the degree of unprecedented flexibility in course content that he needed for his radical approach to succeed. He harnessed it and installed it as the cornerstone of WMG's teaching structure. Alan Curtis, who worked closely with Bhattacharyya for fifteen years as Rover's human resources director and then its manufacturing chief, before joining WMG in 1997, said: 'His great insight was to identify the potential of the module system to deliver what he sought. By making it the standard operating procedure for WMG, he built the whole university–company interface on management modules. That enabled people in jobs to earn diplomas or certificates or final degrees by combining jobs and a module every six months for two and a half years. People could participate in the education programmes and at the same time stay in their jobs.'

The module, as applied and developed by Bhattacharyya and his group, enjoyed its full expression in the Integrated Graduate Development Scheme (IGDS) thanks to Professor Geoffrey Allan and Dr Peter Davies, of the Science and Engineering Research Council (SERC) which agreed to find the scheme in 1982. Again, Bhattacharyya took a commonplace system – in this case, the venerable Teaching Company Scheme – and transformed it by an act of academic alchemy into something innovative and incisive.

For Bhattacharyya, the distinguishing feature of the Teaching Company Scheme was that, by definition, it focused on the company rather than the individual. To this end, he had used the system at the Lucas Institute, with BL's Drews Lane suspension and drive train plant. IGDS – a title redolent of the world of business rather than academia – followed the same principle as the Teaching Company Scheme, but went much, much further. Companies were invited to nominate the graduates they wanted to enrol on the programme, which was to culminate in a Master of Science degree from the University of Warwick. The course – or, in Bhattacharyya's preferred language, the development process – took three years, during which the students continued to be based at their workplace, doing their normal jobs. Half of the credits for the MSc were gained from a dissertation based on a successful project carried out at the student's company. The other half were accumulated from attendance at fourteen one-week residential modules selected from a possible fifty-two modules.

The modules were designed by integrated university–industry teams of specialists. The subjects were agreed by a similarly integrated steering group. They varied from the highly technical to general business management issues. WMG delivered about sixty per cent of the modules, and external 'expert witnesses' delivered the rest. The aim, one senior WMG man said later, was to 'produce an integrated, contributing executive who is conversant with the relevant technology and can manage a business'.

IGDS was the WMG foundation course in another sense. All subsequent teaching programmes, from non-graduate to doctorate, evolved from the scheme, just as Bhattacharyya had derived the IGDS concept from the principle of the Teaching Company Scheme. Through all the applications of the IGDS, Bhattacharyya's precepts remained consistent: 'From the beginning, I said to my customers, "We will train people in such a way that you will immediately get benefit from them." That satisfied the desire of any company to be able to capitalise on the value we had added to their people. I also made it clear that I could decide jointly with the companies the sort of courses they required, and would develop these courses jointly with them.'

This commitment frequently led Bhattacharyya into delicate negotiations with his Senate – not to mention the occasional full-scale battle with outsiders – when Warwick professors and/or engineering institutions objected to the high level of company input and workplace content in what had traditionally been their exclusive preserve. Supported by Butterworth, Bhattacharyya usually won his case. 'Bhattacharyya disregarded the conventional university system. That landed him in all sorts of trouble, but because of his success, he was allowed to operate a profit centre within the university,' said one contemporary. 'Butterworth was always willing to hold off the other institutions and insist that his entrepreneur should have his way.' Both men recognised the battles were worth fighting. Apart from what Bhattacharyya believed to be the superior relevance of the partnership approach, there was also a universal commercial truth: 'When companies agree to use you, they aren't worried about how much money they are paying provided that the problem gets solved,' he said.

Certainly, most of the companies that became clients tended to stay with WMG. BL was the supreme example of such loyalty. Michael James-Moore, who had encountered Bhattacharyya when the Professor was at the Lucas Institute and he was BL's Powertrain Manufacturing Director, was one early client. 'I became Industrial Engineering director at Leyland Cars [as the division encompassing all BL's brands was then named] and used Kumar and his team to do some computer simulation work. He brought two young Indians with him, and one Saturday night I found them working after midnight. They were very keen and very diligent.'

James-Moore was one of the first WMG customers to discover an important truth about Bhattacharyya: 'One of the key things about Warwick was that KB and co. tended to deliver on things,' he recalled. Other managers at both Leyland Cars and Land Rover also appreciated that. When Bhattacharyya launched IGDS, a stream of young, up-and-coming managers from both the car and the four-wheel-drive operations were sent to join the scheme.

James-Moore was impressed: 'Younger people at what became Rover were taking on responsibility earlier. People of my generation were aged forty before we had learned half of what we needed to know, but the Warwick-trained people were doing manufacturing-related work from an early stage. The WMG graduate training was the thing that got it going, because to change the way Rover did things, you had to change the way managers were taught. I would have run factories very differently early in my career had I been through the IGDS.'

James-Moore had no doubt that the critical element of IGDS was its combination of engineering and financial content. 'When I was starting out in management, a lot of the people who ran factories were engineers or engineering-based. We always got shafted by the accountants because we didn't understand their game. They would talk about discounted cash-flow projections and rates of return, and we didn't have an answer. IGDS took the engineers out into a wider field. It enabled them to hold their corner. Everybody learned the language of marketing and finance, which made it possible for engineers to run businesses again.'

BL executives were not alone in taking a shine to Bhattacharyya's work. His twin themes – eliminating the divide between university and industry, and teaching notoriously innumerate British engineers the prerequisites of effective management – caught the eye of Keith Joseph, Mrs Thatcher's first Secretary of State for Industry. Joseph was Thatcher's mentor and the new government's philosopher-king. The American free marketer Milton Friedman may have inspired Thatcherite monetarist economics, but Joseph – author of a celebrated 1976 lecture, *Monetarism is Not Enough* – provided the connection between the theory and the practice. Thatcher only stood for the leadership in 1975 when Joseph decided not to run against Heath. During the years of opposition, he headed the Centre for Policy Studies, the wellspring for the redesign of what Sir John Hoskyns, one of its alumni, called Britain's 'political economy'. Thatcher was the heart of the new regime, but Joseph was its mastermind.

In government, as the man in the eye of the industrial relations storm created by the 1979–80 national steel strike, Joseph became the public face and voice of non-interventionism. He articulated the new credo that it was both the right and the responsibility of management to manage, thereby signalling both the end of the post-war consensus of fudge and mudge and the fact that there would be no Heath-style retreat from stand-on-your-own-feet economics. Many observers, even those favourable to Thatcher, found the posture simplistic: early in 1980, at one conference of industrialists in Newcastle, a journalist repeatedly questioned Joseph about his dictum that there could be no role for government in industrial affairs. How did that compare with the relationship between government and industry in Japan, France, Germany – even the United States? At the end of the day, the exasperated Joseph confronted the reporter: 'You are living in a dream world, my friend,' he sighed, almost sympathetically.

Joseph was, of course, exaggerating to make the Thatcherites' point. He was certainly willing to give credit where it was due, even when government money had made an achievement possible. At a dinner with Sir Michael Edwardes's BL board at Longbridge, after the launch of the Metro, Joseph was suddenly overcome with emotion. 'This is a wonderful thing that you have achieved here,' he said, clearly moved by the vision of a BL revival. The vision proved illusory, but Joseph did not allow the sight of a new BL begging bowl, requesting another infusion of taxpayers' money, to obscure his view of the work being done to modernise BL's management and processes. His gaze soon alighted on Bhattachar-yya.

Apart from industry, Joseph's great interest was education – after two years at Industry, he became Education Secretary in September 1981 – so in Bhattacharyya he found a kindred spirit: a free-thinking radical with an outsider's view of the faults (and the virtues) of Britain's industrial character.

In time, Joseph introduced Bhattacharyya to Thatcher. Bhattacharyya's first encounter with the formidable PM was not quite in the Stanley and Livingstone category, but it was memorable enough for the WMG founder. 'Kumar, we have just been in a Cabinet meeting discussing your work,' Thatcher told him. Bhattacharyya was aware that he cut an unlikely figure in Number 10. 'The first time I went up the stairs, I knew that everyone had stopped what they were doing and was watching me,' he recalled. Thatcher, however, knew she had found a fellow radical. The Prime Minister was always on the look-out for independent experts who could provide objective advice, free from self-interest and equally free from the influence of the civil servant mentality that she associated with Britain's post-war decline. Bhattacharyya, independently wealthy and with a plethora of knowledge about manufacturing industry and higher education, fitted this bill perfectly. Thanks to Keith Joseph, Bhattacharyya advised the No. 10 policy team on industry, education and R&D.

His influence was growing in other ways, too. At BL, he and his colleagues progressively expanded the use of their simulation techniques to facilitate product design, development and manufacture. Roy recalled: 'I spent a lot of time in Rover plants around the country. In about 1984/5, I started to formalise this activity into a simulation team. Essentially, we were looking at developing models of manufacturing systems, examining alternatives to see where the weaknesses lay, to understand better different parts of the system and where improvements could be made.'

The focus on simulation was one aspect of Bhattacharyya's conviction that only by applying information technology would Britain have any chance of recovering the competitive ground it had lost to its rivals over decades. 'In the UK, we are all individualists, whereas if you want to produce a robust product everything in the link has to work well,' he said. 'You have to have technology to overcome the problem. We realised that there was one particular way in which Britain could start competing again, and that was by using computers. Technology was our only solution.'

That doctrine was nowhere more relevant than at BL. In the home marketplace, the repository of all Britain's volume car marques was falling well behind its main UK rivals, Ford and Vauxhall. Its factories, despite hefty wedges of government finance for projects such as Metro, epitomised the under-investment in new processes from which British manufacturing suffered. The Metro line was an island of automation in the antiquated sea of labour-intensive equipment that was the Longbridge plant. And the shortcomings of BL's line managers meant that the returns on what investment had taken place were inadequate.

In many respects, Bhattacharyya could not have found a more perfect testbed for the WMG technology and teaching model. To compensate for its shrinking economies of scale and relative lack of resources, BL had to think smarter and move more nimbly than its larger rivals if it was to have a chance of holding its own. Based in the group's West Midlands heartland, with increasingly close links to both BL and its suppliers, he also enjoyed top-level influence through his input to the Prime Minister, the Cabinet Office and the Department of Industry. Most importantly for Bhattacharyya, emerging from the BL ranks was a new generation of senior managers who did not share the 'Give us the money and leave us to spend it' insularity of their predecessors. Some of these executives recognised the importance of independent expert advice, and were ready to welcome it. And once that advice had proved its worth, as WMG's did in simulation for the Maestro and Montego lines, the executives were ready to open up their whole operation to the scrutiny of a trusted confidant, as Bhattacharyya and WMG became.

Modelling Maestro/Montego production was the curtain-raiser for Bhattacharyya's work with BL. The main event, from which numerous other activities developed and into which the ensuing simulation work was suffused, was the group-wide application of Computer Aided Design/Computer Aided Manufacture (Cad/Cam).

In the early 1980s, Cad/Cam usage was still in its infancy in Britain. It was pioneered by research-led organisations, such as the Tyneside-based British Shipbuilding Research Association, but industry in general was slow to take up the new technology. In most companies, drawing boards and slide rules persisted deep into the decade. BL was ahead of the curve, but its use of Cad/Cam was highly fragmented. 'There was a miscellany of Cad/Cam systems right across the company,' said Curtis. 'It was clear that the integration of data was necessary because engineering was centralising. One system had to come.'

Bhattacharyya was asked to undertake a strategic review of the options available. He recommended that BL adopt a system developed by the American firm Computervision and implement it across the group. 'At the time, Computervision was one of the two largest Cad/Cam vendors in the world,' recalled Sandy Moffat, one of WMG's executives. 'This was the start of a very important relationship'. BL and WMG then launched a series of projects, titled Cad 1 to Cad 5, that progressively refined and expanded the application of Cad/Cam in the business. 'The university acted as a training and development centre,' said Curtis. 'Rover was a development site company. So we had the tools up front.'

With Computervision on board, Bhattacharyya was soon moving into the kind of territory that he had set out to occupy from the start. The BL partnership enabled him to relate the IGDS teaching programme to the supremely practical, hands-on experience offered by an ambitious process technology initiative in the workplace. The mutually reinforcing combination was compelling, for both WMG and its clients. It came about by a mixture of sound strategic principle and astute opportunism. Once more, Bhattacharyya made his own luck.

'IGDS at the outset was slanted towards technology,' Moffat said. 'It was about bringing line management up to speed with new aspirations in technology, where industry was going and what it was trying to achieve. Through the IGDS course, we covered the breadth and depth of the manufacturing process. We had corporate strategists, robotics people, finance people, Cad/Cam people. We needed four or five people to support the Cad/Cam side alone. We needed equipment, dedicated facilities. Cad/Cam was very much an emerging technology in those days.'

The cost of the equipment, the dedicated facilities and the specialist staff needed to support the Cad/Cam element of IGDS threatened to become prohibitive. 'The Cad/Cam module was running about twenty times a year,' Moffat said. 'On that basis, we couldn't really support the cost of the facility. So in true KB entrepreneurial fashion, we decided to look at the opportunity of providing training to industrial-based engineers in the appreciation of Cad/Cam.'

The BL project was both a showcase and a laboratory for the combination of IGDS education and practical training. 'IGDS had been very much an educational process,' said Moffat. 'This is Cad/Cam; this is where it fits; this is where you, in managing people dealing with this activity, need to develop. Whereas, when we got to the training side, it was much more about how you put a line in, how you constructed a division, which button to press at the right moment.'

For Bhattacharyya, the Cad/Cam project in BL became a reference point. It created educational, technical and personal links that deepened and widened the areas of expertise for which WMG was respected. Two landmarks in particular were direct results of the partnership. The first was the establishment at Warwick of a centre dedicated to technology development work carried out in close collaboration with companies. The second was BL's K-series engine.

One of Bhattacharyya's aims had been to establish a technical facility separate from the university engineering department that would be integral to the WMG philosophy of corporate partnership. In 1986, he succeeded in persuading Rover – as Sir Graham Day, its new chairman, renamed the group – and Rolls-Royce jointly to fund the construction and equipping of what he called the Advanced Technology Centre (ATC).

The ATC substantiated Bhattacharyya's ideal. It was initially focused on the needs of Rover and Rolls, for whom it brought substantial gains. Curtis said: 'The ATC provided Rover with a development facility and brought together quite a large number of leading-edge, highly qualified university staff. They got the benefit of working on real projects. Rover got the benefit of their input for free. A lot of university staff went into the projects – they covered metals, some electronics, electro-magnetic testing, rapid prototyping most of all. Significant advantage in business process terms came out of that.' Indirect benefits were equally profound: 'People formed networks and relationships,' said Curtis. 'All of these things helped Rover managers to become significantly better at their jobs.'

Gradually, the ATC became a magnet for other companies, some of them Rover and Rolls suppliers that were encouraged to participate. In parallel with the increase in ATC customers, Bhattacharyya and his executives expanded the facility to the point where it was carrying out R&D across the engineering spectrum. Design analysis, stereolithography and tooling, electronics, materials, internal combustion engines and recycling were all brought within its purview. Bhattacharyya stretched his net wide, creating some novel combinations: a project examining how to improve the catalytic converter in order to reduce engine emissions more efficiently involved both Rover and Unilever.

The most high-profile, long-lasting and influential project on which Bhattacharyya and the ATC staff worked was also an engine programme. Its origins pre-dated the foundation of the ATC; indeed, the project was conceived inside BL, long before Day's arrival and without Bhattacharyya's initial involvement.

In the early 1980s, BL executives and engineers recognised that, while they had poured money into the M cars, the engines that powered those vehicles were on their last legs. The engine is the most important component of a new car, and not just for the obvious reason. An engine, more than any single element, can define the vehicle, delineate its character, and dictate its potency in the market. Honda and BMW owe the strength of their brands, first and foremost, to the quality of their engine technology. Such is the level of investment, in both design and tooling, required for a new engine range that manufacturers build engines that can be developed for at least two generations of vehicles, and frequently more. The BL engines had reached the end of the road. There was no way that they could be stretched to power the Maestro and Montego successors, and nor would they be adequate for the Metro when that car was updated, as it had to be.

So BL desperately needed a new engine family for its small and medium-sized cars (the next large car, to be known as the Rover 800, was to buy its engines from BL's partner Honda). That engine family had to be capable of wide application. To meet the growing pressures for fuel economy, it had to be lightweight. But it had to be relatively simple, and therefore cost-effective, to build. Rover did not have the money to fund a complex, intricate product.

The BL engineers decided that, if they were to come close to realising their aspirations, they would have to take a calculated risk: they would have to bypass conventional engine design and take a leap into the relatively unknown. They opted for a high-tolerance, thin-wall aluminium structure. They called it the K-series. But they were not sure how to make it sufficiently robust for mass manufacture over an extended period. So they turned to the outfit that had already performed excellent service: they asked Bhattacharyya for advice.

Bhattacharyya and his executives, including Rajat Roy and Gordon Smith, a WMG expert in lightweight materials, immediately recognised what the K-series engine could mean, for both BL and Warwick. For BL, it meant that, if successful, the product would become the reference project for Bhattacharyya's technology effort. The origin of Bhattacharyya's mission had been his diagnosis that Britain lacked a technical base. He had set out to apply information technology as a short cut to close the competitive gap and make the creation of that base possible. And here was something that, utilising that computer technology, could become a pillar of the new industrial base that the Thatcherite revolution hoped to establish. For WMG, as much as for its client, the K-series was a lot more than a showpiece; it was a cornerstone.

'The K-series was the result of a company trying to get into very modern design and looking for innovative techniques to manufacture novel structures,' said Alan Curtis. 'It was a classic instance of collaboration between the university and the company to produce a technical solution that the company would never have thought of by itself, and which the university could never have accomplished without the sponsorship of the company.'

For two years, Bhattacharyya and BL deployed the gamut of Cad/Cam expertise that they had accumulated over their years of co-operation. They used the simulation techniques in which both parties were now well versed. But where simulation had previously been applied to the fairly conventional task of virtually rehearsing a new model introduction, this time it was allied to revolutionary design. For ease and low cost of manufacture, to minimise machining time and the risk of defects, Bhattacharyya and the BL engineers devised a compact engine block with one unique feature. The K-series was held together not by a number of small bolts inserted at different points and angles as in conventional engines, but by a single long bolt running diagonally across the block.

Like all great innovations, the concept was ingenious, but simple. The big question was whether it would come off: would the engine hold together under the intense pressures of mass manufacture and long-term usage? It would not have been the first time that an apparently brilliant BL drawing-board design had crumbled in production: Rover's superb-looking SD1 had lost all credibility when drivers found that its transmission repeatedly fell apart. Collective memories of such disasters died hard, even among those who inherited, rather than participated in them. During the death throes of the Rover SD1, Graham Day had been trying to salvage British Shipbuilders. But when Thatcher appointed him to succeed Sir Austin Bide as BL's chairman in 1986, Day quickly cross-examined Bhattacharyya about the K-series. 'Kumar,' asked the agitated chairman, 'are you sure this is going to work?' Bhattacharyya was confidence personified. He assured Day that it would. But even he was not certain of success.

Day's conversation with Bhattacharyya, and what became Rover's K-series triumph, almost never happened. In late 1985, Ford had begun secret talks with the government about taking over the cars side of what was still called BL. In parallel, General Motors was holding discussions about buying Land Rover and BL's truck business. The twin-track negotiations were initiated by the Thatcher administration, which had concluded that a division and sale of the BL operations to much bigger and more powerful competitors offered the only alternative to continued large-scale subsidy of the creaking company. If BL stayed where it was, 99.4 per cent owned by, and 100 per cent dependent on the state, then taxpayers' money would either continue to be poured into a black hole of sustained losses, or would have to be used to liquidate the business, with unacceptable employment and political consequences.

The Thatcher conclusion was informed and guided by Bhattacharyya's own close-up view of BL. To Bhattacharyya, it was clear that BL as it stood had no chance of recovering the ground it had lost to its foreign-owned rivals. The other option, to do what the French government had done in pumping vast sums into Renault, was not an option for BL, Bhattacharyya believed. France was effectively a closed car market controlled by a duopoly, Renault and Peugeot-Citroën; Britain was a free market where BL was already a poor third. Moreover, as Bhattacharyya knew very well, BL's management was inferior to the French. It needed the kind of sustained upgrade that the Warwick IGDS was designed to help achieve. In short, to have any hope of reversing its long-term decline, Bhattacharyya believed, the business needed a big brother with the financial and technical resources necessary to engineer a turnround. Even Land Rover, despite its pre-eminence in the European four-wheel-drive market, could not run on a shoestring indefinitely. Eventually, Bhattacharyya believed, it was bound to be challenged by the Japanese and the Americans in its own backyard. It, too, could only survive and prosper in the long term under the umbrella of a multinational group. His views struck a chord with Thatcher, who was nothing if not a realist, who had no hang-ups about foreign ownership of British companies and who had already championed Japanese car-makers' inward investment into the UK.

Bhattacharyya's influence on the Ford negotiations in particular was more than a high-level affair of state. It was equally strong at the technical level, literally in the engine room. For Ford, one of the prime attractions of the deal was to acquire the K-series technology. The Americans were acutely aware that they had neglected their own engine development programmes and, with a new Escort under development and due for production in four years' time, were badly in need of a modern power plant that could be extended into a full engine family. They recognised from the outset that the K-series was the answer to their problems. Bhattacharyya found himself influencing the Ford–BL plan from two directions: top-down and bottom-up.

In the end, both the Ford and GM deals were run off the road by the Westland crisis. The crisis temporarily weakened Thatcher's authority and prevented her from driving through the deals against backbench opposition by West Midlands Tory MPs abetted by senior BL executives. The opposition was myopic, and led to the still more damaging refusal of the government in 1987 to contemplate selling Rover to Volkswagen, whose chairman Carl Hahn was keen to acquire the company.

For Bhattacharyya, however, the events produced more positive consequences. They were a landmark in Warwick's development, testifying both to the credibility that Bhattacharyya had gained at the highest levels of government and to the relevance of WMG's technical input on its industrial homeground. That influence was now bound to increase, because the failure of the discussions meant both that BL had to develop a credible semi-independent strategy, bolstered only by its partnership with Honda, and that it was even more vital for the K-series to be brought successfully into production.

After Thatcher brought in Day to replace the BL executives who had opposed the Ford and GM sales, Bhattacharyya established a close relationship with the new regime at Rover: Day, George Simpson, who ran Leyland Trucks before emerging as Day's first lieutenant, Rob Meakin, the personnel director, and Andy Barr, the principal survivor of the pre-Day era, who headed manufacturing operations.

The Bhattacharyya–Barr partnership stimulated a series of far-sighted initiatives that not only benefited Rover, but created a shop-window for WMG's philosophy of technology management. In the straitened circumstances where Rover now found itself, there was no room for prejudice and preconception. The focus was on survival, and on finding people who could contribute to that bare essential. In this fertile soil, the decades-old Berlin Wall between industry and higher education came tumbling down. Bhattacharyya had found a ready receptacle for his unique vision.

There was no guinea-piggery about WMG's approach to Rover. The partnership was intensely realistic and pragmatic. But it was also ambitious – it put in place shopfloor management practices that were unprecedented in hidebound British industry. Bhattacharyya would never claim total responsibility for the changes that Rover made – the Honda influence on Rover cars was fundamental – but

37

WMG played a central role as a facilitator, in equipping the Rover management to understand the Japanese methods and to translate them to Rover's own production systems.

This requirement hugely expanded Bhattacharyya's Rover constituency. If the company really was going to achieve a paradigm shift in production efficiency, the re-education effort would have to extend well beyond Rover's graduate engineers. Beside the IGDS, Bhattacharyya needed something else, a programme for middle managers in general.

The man who helped him find the answer was, ironically, himself a former BL manager. Clive Reynolds joined WMG in 1987 from Leyland Trucks, where Simpson and Meakin had cut their teeth. Before that, he had been with W.S. Atkins, the consulting engineer. He therefore combined an insider's understanding of Rover with the consultant's objectivity and wider experience. Reynolds took over the running of the IGDS, on which a stream of Rover engineers were now engaged each year. And he and Bhattacharyya introduced a new programme, which they called the Integrated Management Development Scheme (IMDS). 'That got the middle managers started,' said Reynolds. 'It was a huge breakthrough.'

The Warwick IMDS, Curtis believed, was a prerequisite for Rover's manufacturing reformation. 'It was as important as anything in the changes we made throughout our plants. Rover manufacture became all about the autonomous cell. The manufacturing people who had been used to foremen and charge hands and telling people what to do were changed to team leaders and cell working. We knew about the principle of cellular manufacture from Honda. But there were no Honda people in Rover – there was no guidance from them on how to do it, so we had to find our own way. That was where WMG's role was crucial.'

With Barr, Bhattacharyya developed a series of other initiatives to enable Rover managers to adopt Japanese best practice. The Japanese were renowned for working with suppliers to improve performance and cut costs, rather than merely trying to squeeze the last penny of a price cut out of them, as the Americans did. Warwick devised a Partnership Sourcing programme, which put 200 purchasing managers at Rover through a series of modules that shifted them from the adversarial approach to the much broader business perspective required by partnership sourcing. In tandem, Bhattacharyya helped Barr identify 150–200 of Rover's suppliers as 'preferred suppliers' to spearhead the change to partnership.

Under WMG's aegis, Rover established a manufacturing policy unit at Warwick, staffed by three young Rover graduates and supported by about sixty university staff. 'We shall be thinking about the whole manufacturing strategy,' Barr said at the time. 'We want free thinking; we mustn't have contaminated thinking. We can't have people saying, "You can't do that because it won't happen".' It was a ringing endorsement of Bhattacharyya's iconoclastic manufacturing philosophy.

Bhattacharyya continued to work with Rover for most of the 1990s, through the period of its ownership by BMW. But in some respects the WMG-assisted revolution at Rover reached its full flowering with the launch of the first of the R8 cars, the original Rover 200, in 1989. By then, Bhattacharyya had been working with Rover for almost a decade, and the 200 production line at Longbridge displayed many of the results of their collaboration. There were no foremen on the line, and the layers of management on the project were cut from Rover's usual five to three. Production was cellular, and the system revolved around mini-managing directors – production managers with responsibility for 80–100 workers and complete authority and accountability for work in their area. Thanks to the IT systems Rover had introduced with WMG's help, all the data the managers needed to support informed decision-making was at their fingertips. Most were in their twenties or early thirties, veterans of the IGDS or IMDS programmes at Warwick. A significant number were women, which only helped to encourage their nickname: 'Barr's Babes'.

Nonetheless, the guiding hand behind the shopfloor reorganisa-
tion was that of Bhattacharyya. It was he who had turned
conventional Western vehicle manufacturing thinking on its head by
devising a modular system. 'The fundamental mistake of American
and European manufacturers has been to go for more and more
capacity,' he said. 'Then, because of variations in demand, they
haven't been able to utilise that capacity. All car-makers have
excess capacity, and that costs a lot of money. The Japanese do it
differently. They go for the sort of capacity that can be utilised and
then add to it when demand increases.'

That was the new thinking that Bhattacharyya implanted in
Rover. It was an imperfect operation, because Longbridge was
lumbered with the huge installed overhead of bygone production
levels, something it never succeeded in shaking off. But the Rover
200 line bucked the general Longbridge model, and the nearby K-
series production unit was an abiding showpiece for Bhattacharyya's
convictions.

Here, in all its unlikely glory, was the aluminium casting process
that WMG had helped Rover develop, replete with its weight-
saving and thermodynamic efficiency. Here was a fully automated
production line, studded with robots and lasers, where value
engineering reigned supreme. Rover's limited investment resources
had been concentrated on conrod, crankshaft and shell-bearing
manufacture – the components that dictate engine quality.
Machining centres and melt furnaces alike were divided into
clusters of cells, giving Rover the flexibility to modulate capacity in
line with demand. More than a decade later, long after the Rover
200 had receded into distant memory, long after Rover's ambitions
to become a world-leading brand had come to dust, the K-series
line lived on, a working monument to Bhattacharyya's manufacturing revolution.

Chapter Three
Going Global

One morning in late 1987, a captain of British manufacturing industry walked into 10, Downing Street for an important meeting with the Prime Minister. The chief executive concerned, who for confidentiality reasons must remain anonymous even this number of years on, was primed for a tough debate. The particular issue involved was highly sensitive, and the executive knew that he would have to marshal some powerful arguments to persuade Mrs Thatcher that his views on the subject should prevail.

Entering the meeting-room, the industrialist was surprised to find that his audience included not only Thatcher and her close officials, but a mysterious addition to the Prime Minister's team, someone whom he had never seen before. The man seemed quite at home, sitting on a sofa and frequently responding to Mrs Thatcher's invitations to comment. After being cross-examined about his views, the somewhat chastened executive returned to his head office. 'Who was there?' one of his colleagues asked him. 'Mrs Thatcher, her people and some Indian', he replied.

The executive had just become one of the first industrialists to gain an insight into the influential role being played by Bhattacharyya as Thatcher's independent adviser on industrial matters. By the time of this particular audience at Number 10, Bhattacharyya was well-established as an authority with the PM's ear. According to Peter Warrie, a former member of Mrs Thatcher's Policy Unit, Bhattacharyya's views were sought on a range of matters: 'There was the motor industry, but also innovation policy, education and other manufacturing issues. It was quite useful to say to Mrs T: "This is also Kumar's view" on a particular topic'. Warrie, who later joined WMG, kept an open line to Bhattacharyya, whose meetings with Thatcher became less frequent: 'He would bump into her three or four times a year,' Warrie recalled. 'Undoubtedly, however, he had an influence over decision-making in these areas.'

The outside world saw nothing of this influence, chiefly because Bhattacharyya never advertised the fact. He always recognised that the value attributed to his input and the trust vested in him stood in inverse proportion to the level of his public profile. The lower the latter, the greater the weight he carried in councils of state. Every so often, his advice fed through into some headline-grabbing event. In September 1989, the Ford Motor Company launched a tender offer to buy 14.9 per cent of Jaguar, the first shot in a bid to take control of the Coventry-based luxury car-maker. The next day, Thatcher endorsed Ford's bid: Ford, she said, 'would be a good owner for Jaguar'. A month later, against the wishes of the Trade and Industry Secretary Nicholas Ridley, the government removed the 'golden share' that it held in Jaguar to prevent a hostile takeover of the company. The move enabled Ford to buy the company for £1.6 billion – a price, incidentally, that it came to regret, but which delivered enormous value to Jaguar shareholders.

That, however, was not Thatcher's intention. Months earlier, she had reached the conclusion – counselled by Bhattacharyya – that Jaguar was sliding into difficulties, with sales and profits tumbling, and would become a political issue unless a big car company took it over. This time, she was determined that there should be no repetition of the abortive 1985–6 BL sale attempt. The action taken was decisive and, to a degree, ruthless. But the mission was accomplished. As a potential political issue, Jaguar was neutralised overnight.

The Jaguar case highlighted Bhattacharyya's value to the Prime Minister. He brought to the situation local knowledge – the company was headquartered just down the road from WMG – a deep understanding of the car industry, an international perspective and, above all, a view that was objective and disinterested. Thatcher was so impressed with his judgement that she later asked him to take out British citizenship so that he could gain the requisite access to advise on defence-related industrial issues.

Bhattacharyya's relationship with the Thatcher government remained a closely guarded secret for its duration. It would, of course, have been a wonderful calling card for WMG, especially in the organisation's early days. But, while remaining ever-alert to expansion opportunities, Bhattacharyya followed a measured, methodical strategy for developing his business.

From his standing start in 1981, with a staff of twelve and total income of £700,000 in his first full year of operation, Bhattacharyya grew WMG over the next five years to a staff of sixty-five and total income of £8m, split almost equally between research and teaching. By 1991, he had more than doubled the size of the group again. WMG now had 154 staff and that year income totalled £20m. He now stood on the threshold of the most dramatic expansion phase in WMG's short history.

For all the radicalism of his concept and the innovative paths to growth that he pursued, this expansion strategy was in many respects classical in its form. Thus, he graduated from the initial basic teaching company-type work into fully fledged joint research projects with complete two-way flow between WMG and its clients. Similarly, he initially established WMG's reputation through his work in the motor industry, centred on BL. From there, he gradually migrated into other sectors, broadening the customer base into the aerospace, pharmaceuticals, electronics – both hardware and software – electricity and construction industries.

The vehicles that carried WMG into this spectrum of engineering- and manufacturing-related sectors were the IGDS and IMDS programmes. Clive Reynolds said: 'IGDS established us – we had well over a hundred graduates a year through to 1995. IMDS got the middle managers started. That was the huge breakthrough. Behind those schemes, we had a second generation of derivative programmes, such as engineering for non-engineers at Lucas. The concept was to teach engineering to the finance personnel in such a way that they could contribute to an engineering business.'

London Electricity exemplified the diversification made possible by IMDS. The company was created from the old London Electricity Board as one of the twelve regional electricity companies privatised in 1990. London's directors decided that their senior managers needed schooling in the competitive disciplines of the private sector. 'London was massive,' Reynolds said. 'They wanted to know what the management thinking was in a modern industrial world, and they concluded that the manufacturing systems route, not the MBA route, was the best means of learning that.'

Most significantly of all, Bhattacharyya progressively transformed WMG from almost exclusive concentration on the British market to truly international operation. In the process, he anticipated – and in his own context pioneered – the trend that dominated the 1990s: 'I realised that the UK is a small country and that you couldn't generate a large amount of revenues there,' said Bhattacharyya. 'So I globalised.'

Students from overseas had been attending WMG courses almost from the group's inception. But this was consistent with the decades-old pattern in which thousands of foreign students, such as

Bhattacharyya himself, travelled to Britain for postgraduate education or work experience. By contrast, the decision to establish centres of excellence overseas was a huge departure from the historic norm. It was, however, an entirely logical extension of Bhattacharyya's ethos of going to meet the customers in their own backyard rather than passively awaiting their arrival on the domestic doorstep.

Bhattacharyya's focus was Asia, where he recognised that the fast-developing 'Tiger' economies had a clear and present need for the engineering business management approach. The most pressing demand for WMG's services came, however, from the region's longest-established economy.

In the late eighties, Hong Kong's financial services industry was buoyant, but its once-thriving manufacturing sector was suffering from a combination of factors that threatened to trigger a meltdown. Since the 1984 Joint Declaration by China and Britain clearing the way for the return of sovereignty to the People's Republic, there had been a growing brain drain from the colony which had sapped its resources of qualified middle and senior managers. At the same time, manufacturers were emigrating to cheaper sources of land and labour in the region – in the Philippines and Malaysia, but above all across the border into the Pearl River delta around Guangzhou in mainland China. Thirdly, the manufacturers were being squeezed by the fast-growing economies of Japan, Singapore and South Korea.

Hong Kong's City fathers were alarmed at the exodus of managers and factories. They recognised the continued importance of manufacturing to the economy, part of whose bedrock was the 800,000 workers in 50,000 small firms producing a host of components for the handful of large groups that dominated manufacturing activity. The Hong Kong government and a group of financial institutions instigated an effort to reverse the manufacturing decline. They wanted a higher education programme that could upgrade the skills of Hong Kong's abundant population of technical staff whose qualifications fell short of degree level. The enhanced and expanded managerial cadre would then be capable of meeting the challenge of moving manufacturing in the colony up the value chain and developing its intellectual property.

Hong Kong's need was answered perfectly by Bhattacharyya's engineering business management approach. In 1989, WMG forged a joint venture with Hong Kong Polytechnic (now the Polytechnic University) to create the Business and Technology Centre (BTC) under the direction of Professor John Hearn. The following year, the Polytechnic began to teach the Integrated Graduate Development Scheme, with regular input from visting WMG lectures. The course got off to a roaring start with more than 200 students, and the number increased from there.

Hearn said later: 'Before 1980, Hong Kong had only two uiversities and two polytechnics. Not many people had the opportunity of receiving university education, especially in engineering. As a result, there was a backlog of very able and enthusiastic, but unqualified technical staff working in manufacturing industries. The IGDS was introduced with two aims: the upgrading of staff to MSc level with a high quality, practical programme and, secondly, the retention of those professionals in Hong Kong for at least three years while they were on the course.'

Twelve 'founder member' manufacturers financed the Centre, ranging from CIM Systems, a computer networking company, through HAECO, the Hong Kong aircraft engine servicing company to Wah Shing Toys. Henry Tseng, chief executive of another founder member, the telecoms equipment maker Kingtronics, decided to set an example to his staff by joining the programme. Tseng overcame a modest schooling in China to emerge with distinction from the degree course. Another of the founder members was the the machine tool maker Chen Hsong Holdings, whose director Dr K.P. Pau enrolled as a student and did a PhD in noise pollution. Thus inspired, he co-founded a company called Eco-Tek, specialising in environmental control.

The programme, which was soon expanded to encompass the Integrated Management Development Scheme, was supremely well-suited to the most critical issue facing manufacturers in Hong Kong: how to manage the relocation of their basic operations to cheaper areas, notably China, while retaining at base both overall control and value-adding activities such as design and marketing. Hearn said: 'The relocation of labour-intensive activities into China resulted in a major shift of management requirement from a local, technological-orientated approach to an engineering services and systems approach for remote control of manufacturing capability on the mainland. Hong Kong thus changed from essentially local manufacturing to a design and logistics control base for operations in China. The IGDS course proved to be the ideal vehicle to equip managers for this transformation, particularly when localised with the help of senior industrialists and academics working together as a genuine partnership.'

Just as at Warwick itself, the programme gradually spread its wings into service-related sectors. Through word of mouth, IGDS became the preferred MSc level course. 'This was the first time in Hong Kong that an education programme had been launched in full partnership with industry,' Hearn recalled in 2002. 'This model has now been adopted in many other facets of the Polytechnic University's activities.' Over the decade that they have been involved with the course, some of the founder members enjoyed spectacular growth with their firms more than trebling in size. 'Many of my students have become multi-millionaires; some are now billionaires,' said Bhattacharyya with pride.

The emergence of Hong Kong as the prototype for WMG's overseas expansion was partly a happy accident – Bhattacharyya happened to find a local grouping that was receptive to his aims. But it also owed much to design: Bhattacharyya was very aware that Hong Kong was the gateway to what could be by far his largest potential market: the People's Republic of China.

Bhattacharyya's links with China went back to his childhood: on a visit to New York with his father, he met Chou En-Lai, the Chinese Premier. The encounter provided an early instance of Bhattacharyya's insatiable curiosity, his refusal to be overawed in any company, and his determination to speak his mind. Chou conducted the conversation in Chinese, even though he was known to speak very good English. So at the end of the meeting, the young Kumar simply asked him: 'Why didn't you speak English?' Chou was highly amused.

In the early nineties, WMG was not yet ready for the huge challenge that mainland China represented – and China was not ready for WMG. Other states in South-East Asia, however, were keen to establish links with Warwick. First came Malaysia: with the Malaysian University of Technology, WMG set up a centre in Kuala Lumpur for research and post-graduate education in engineering business management. The venture was closely modelled on the Hong Kong structure, but the political dimension was more important. Thanks partly to an introduction provided by Mrs Thatcher, Bhattacharyya established a close relationship with the autocratic Malaysian Prime Minister, Mahathir Mohamad. With Mahathir's support and encouragement, the WMG chairman launched the IGDS programme in 1992. Take-up was slow initially, but accelerated after Dr. Ahmed Zaharudin Idrus was appointed vice-chancellor of the university in June 1994.

Dr. Idrus was a former executive of the state-owned oil group Petronas. With a background in both industry and academia, he understood precisely the advantages conferred by the Bhattacharyya approach. Like Britain, Malaysia had suffered from a discrepancy between the output from universities and the needs of industry. 'In the past, academics looked at things from a very different perspective,' Idrus said. 'We wanted a partnership between government, industry and university.'

Apart from educating about 200 students a year in IGDS and IMDS, the Centre also helped lay the foundations of initiatives in the late nineties that intensified the triple alliance. Backed by

Mahathir, Idrus took charge of MIGHT – the Malaysian Industry Group for Higher Technology – before, in 2002, being appointed Science Adviser to the Prime Minister.

Almost all the major groups active in Malaysia – both domestic manufacturers such as Proton, the car company, and large inward investors such as Motorola – participated in MIGHT. As with WMG in Britain, work with smaller companies was a particularly important element in the partnership with Warwick: 'This has helped us provide education in terms of technology and business management for small and medium-sized enterprises,' said Idrus. 'That is very important for the transformation of Malaysia from a supply chain standpoint.' Bhattacharyya said: 'Malaysia has plenty of good businessmen, but it is now entering the second stage of its development. It needs technology push, but it also needs technology pull – the technology can come from anywhere in the world, but it is essential to ensure that people are aware of it and understand how to harness it for innovation.'

After Malaysia came Thailand. Bhattacharyya formed an academia–business partnership with Chulalongkorn University in Bangkok and the Federation of Thai Industries to create the Regional Centre for Manufacturing Systems Engineering, combining research and postgraduate education.

In India, Bhattacharyya's network and his long-time work with several large Indian companies were formalised in November 1994 in an alliance between WMG and the Confederation of Indian Industries to establish a technology centre in Calcutta funded by business. WMG's Indian work was wide-ranging: it extended from Bombay Dyeing, a textile company, to Tafe, a Madras tractor company, and from TVS Suzuki, a motorbike manufacturer just outside Bhattacharyya's home city of Bangalore, to Telco, an engineering and locomotive maker which is part of the giant Tata conglomerate.

Under the umbrella of Bhattacharyya's extensive contacts, the Indian work was run by Curtis with Stan Mendham, who had joined

WMG after working with Curtis at Land Rover in the later 1980s. Mendham also ran Rover's Gaydon test centre and was seconded to the DTI before moving to Warwick. In India, he worked in several of the companies, helping them to put in place robust engineering processes that promoted quality.

'Because India had been a closed market for so long, indigenous companies lacked the experience of world-class practices in the engineering process,' Curtis said. 'We have shown the companies how to plan their business further than just one year at a time; how to deliver improvement based on using manufacturing strategies; how to organise project and process improvement activities; how to identify the right people and the competences to go with that improvement process across the manufacturing, engineering, sales and marketing disciplines.' A milestone was WMG's work with Tata as the group developed Indicar, the first car to be indigenously designed and manufactured for the Indian market. Before the vehicle's launch in 1999, every car built in India was under licence using a foreign company's design. In 2002, in recognition for his contribution to the country's economic development, Bhattacharyya was accorded India's supreme honour, the Jewel of India. Of his many awards and accolades, this, understandably, was received with the greatest pride.

In 1995, Bhattarcharyya secured the breakthrough into China for which had been hoping ever since he first concluded his partnership in Hong Kong. The pivotal player was Mr Chiang, a successful Hong Kong entrepreneur who established a charitable foundation, the Chiang foundation, funded by dividends from shares he had vested in a trust. The foundation paid for twenty Chinese engineering and manufacturing company executives to attend WMG for ten-week courses which combined teaching, industrial visits and language improvement – along with some sightseeing. At the end of the period, they received a diploma in engineering and manufacturing strategy.

The Chiang visits continued until late 1998, by which time a hundred Chinese executives a year had been able to take the Warwick diploma course. But then came the Asian crisis, when economies across the region melted down, sending a shiver through world stock markets and confounding all the bullish forecasts of untrammelled Asian expansion for years to come.

In Hong Kong, the stock market plunged – drastically reducing the dividend flow from the Chiang foundation to the point where funding in 1999 for the WMG visits had to be limited to one visit of twenty executives. But the storm cloud had a truly silver lining. On the Warwick lecturing and research staff was a Shanghai man with valuable government contacts. Through his good offices, WMG was able to open a dialogue with Safea, the Chinese State Administration for Foreign Export Affairs, which regulates all overseas visits of Chinese business personnel. Safea had great respect for the WMG/Chiang programme. Some of the early participants had since risen to senior executive or even ministerial level.

To sustain the programme, Safea agreed to sponsor sixty executives to visit in 1999. Bhattacharyya, Curtis and their Shanghai colleague flew to Beijing to sign the official agreement. It was quite an event. The Safea director was of senior ministerial level, and part of the Safea complex of buildings was a large hotel. The Safea people asked Bhattacharyya whether he had ever stayed there before. Indeed he had, Bhattacharyya replied. He had been a guest in 1976, when he was helping to train Chinese engineers working on the country's new aerospace programme. Bhattacharyya was the only foreigner to attend the firing of the Mao Long March missile. With credentials like that, the WMG delegation's success was assured. The agreement was signed, and in 2000, Safea repeated its support for the programme. 'We got a better population for the programme because Safea were involved,' said Curtis. The applicants were processed through Wuhan University, where they were screened for minimum standards of English. Safea encouraged WMG to develop closer links with the university. The connection, allied with Safea's sponsorship, could enable WMG to set up programmes at Wuhan.

Bhattacharyya was already pursuing other roads into China. Alongside the Chiang initiative had come another relationship resulting from the Hong Kong connection. Through John Hearn's good offices, a link was established between Warwick and Nanjing University, which was sited in one of the cluster areas for China's nascent vehicle-making industry. Two years later, in 1997, WMG responded to an invitation from the DTI's automotive division to join a mission to China, designed to pass on lessons Britain had learned in resuscitating vehicle-making here. The mission was repeated the following March. Several British universities partici-pated, and Alan Curtis represented Warwick.

The missionaries visited Shanghai and Beijing, but Curtis focused on Nanjing. Along with a counterpart from the University of Birmingham, he returned there eight months later to assess the capability of the automotive supply industry in the area and benchmark it against world standards. They visited nine motor component makers and reported what they found to the Chinese. 'It was a fairly hard-hitting report,' Curtis recalled. 'They had quite good kit, but it was standing idle. And the general state of maintenance and process control was terrible.'

Curtis thought the honesty of the report might not be very good policy for WMG's Chinese ambitions: 'We thought the report would get us turfed out pretty quickly, but it didn't. They asked us to make proposals for launching a centre-of-excellence program-me.' The idea was to take Chinese engineering graduates to British universities and then send them back to Chinese companies where they could bring their learning to bear and raise standards. However, the plan quickly ran into problems: to work, the Nanjing campuses needed money to sponsor engineers to come to Britain, money that was not available in either China or Britain. 'Probably the only way we will be able to get this going is if a British company decides to locate in Nanjing,' said Curtis.

Nanjing remains the original satellite centre for WMG in mainland China, but it is no longer the only one. In 1999, through an agreement between the People's Republic and the Hong Kong Young Industrialist Council, WMG established a centre at the Research Insitute of Tsinghua University, China's leading university, in Shenzen. The following year, a similar centre was set up at the Hua Zhong University of Technology in Wuhan. Hearn said: 'These initiatives, together with the Chiang Foundation training programme, give WMG probably the highest profile of any overseas university operating in China within the manufacturing area.' The group has also established itself in Shanghai, where Bhattacharyya's Chinese contacts again proved invaluable. He had already forged an excellent relationship with Mr Wu, the Chinese education minister who was a former mayor of Shanghai, and through him Bhattacharyya and Curtis got to know his successor. The mayor encouraged them to work with Shanghai University. Given the vibrancy of the region as a commercial and financial centre, the potential for development was clear. In time, Shanghai could be even bigger for WMG than Hong Kong.

'I think that we have got a good foundation in China,' said Curtis. 'Having Safea's backing is really important and the personal links in Shanghai are significant. It may take five or ten years, but the Chinese operations will have substantial programme volume and be large revenue earners. The market is huge beyond belief, but at the moment the Chinese are not used to paying Western costs of air travel or consultancy fees. The more we can do to teach our programmes in China to save travel costs, the faster we'll grow the market.'

While Warwick's overseas operations expanded through the 1990s, the challenges at home became more complex and exacting. 'In terms of education efficiency in the early and mid-nineties, we did ever so well,' said Clive Reynolds. 'The UK programmes were humming along. The overseas programmes were in place. But having got all that, Kumar and I started worrying about the business effectiveness of what we had developed.'

53

Their concerns were compounded by evidence of a puzzling tail-off in demand for the courses. 'It was a very difficult time for us,' recalled Reynolds. 'We knew, because we were measuring all the time, that the core programmes were running better than ever before. Initially, it was a mystery why people weren't registering for them. The companies didn't say that they were fed up. We knew that the people weren't fed up.'

Reynolds focused first on the IMDS. 'We had taken the scales from people's eyes,' he said. 'The middle managers loved coming here and getting a chance to think through the framework for their jobs. They were understanding finance for the first time, understanding IT. Yet we would give them projects to do, and they would do them – some well, others not so well.

'The difference between anecdotal benefit, of which we had evidence in plenty, and actual demonstrable benefit began to worry me a lot,' Reynolds said. 'Demonstrable benefit was really hard to find. You could get a project or a deal like London Electricity, which produced clear improvement, and that was terrific. But usually, companies couldn't have a direct enough relationship with the programmes.'

And that factor, Reynolds concluded, also lay at the heart of the reduction in demand for programmes. 'For the companies, it was a question of releasing people after the 1990–2 recession. There was less manpower, so companies simply couldn't afford to release people for programmes that didn't bring demonstrable benefit. The client needed to see, if he was going to spend £X,000 on a WMG course, that his business would benefit. The issue for me was how we could better demonstrate that benefit. I talked about it with Kumar. He said: "Great, go and do it."'

Reynolds and Bhattacharyya realised that the early 1990s recession had created a watershed in the development of management education and, by extension, in the evolution of WMG. During the 1980s, Bhattacharyya's pioneering, industry-friendly approach had struck a chord among the corporate survivors of the 1980–2 slump. In the uncertain industrial climate that followed the early eighties recession, companies had lost the familiar bearings of the discredited post-war consensus. A whole generation of top management, and a number of historic corporate names, were washed away in the Thatcher revolution. Their successors, liberated into a brave but daunting new world, cast around for suitable landmarks and frames of reference.

Bhattacharyya's particular genius was not only to identify this nebulous need but to devise a model that satisfied it. He did what all outstanding entrepreneurs succeed in doing: he converted latent and ill-formed wants into a market that he defined. Companies knew they needed help to upgrade the quality of their managerial corps, but they could not begin to articulate what kind of help they needed. Bhattacharyya and his WMG colleagues provided a set of specific signposts under the engineering business management umbrella, made user-friendly by the modular, empirical approach.

But for all its responsiveness, its emphasis on collaboration and its sensitivity to the needs of the customer, this approach was still, in many respects, prescriptive. IGDS and IMDS were templates handed down by Warwick to its grateful customers. Since the companies had no other experience, except that of decades of dealing with universities that seemed to be on a different planet, they gladly took what they were offered. It was a learning decade.

Ten years on, the early nineties recession brought this formative period to an end. For many companies, carried away by the volumetric excess of the eighties boom, the events of 1990–2 marked a rude awakening. On the other side of that recession, they emerged with a determination to put what they had learned about management education in the 1980s to better use. Before, take-up of the WMG programmes had been indiscriminate: companies were simply delighted that the schemes were available. Now, this indiscriminate response suddenly became more discriminating. Companies had served their apprenticeship during the eighties. Bhattacharyya was now dealing with a more sophisticated corporate clientele for whom generic courses were no longer enough, even the highly relevant kind of generic courses offered by WMG. Companies now knew what they wanted: tailor-made programmes that answered precise needs and filled specific gaps in the capabilities of their managers. It was not quite a question of quality superseding quantity – the quality of WMG's programmes had not been in doubt. But companies now wanted a different kind of quality – the difference between a high-quality standard product and a higher value-added product.

This was a challenge for Bhattacharyya and co., but it was also a vindication. Faced with such a sea-change in demand, many institutions would have floundered. But the WMG partnership ethos meant that the group was well positioned to respond to the changed mood and the new requirement.

Reynolds was alert to the challenge. His thinking about how to meet it was stimulated one day by John Ferrie, head of Rolls-Royce's civil aero-engines business, who championed the Warwick IMDS in the privatised engineering group. 'John Ferrie asked me a question about the relationship between a particular part of IMDS and something the company was doing,' recalled Reynolds. 'I couldn't really answer him satisfactorily within the framework that we had adopted. So I had to look at various other approaches. The obvious way was to create a more specific link between the objectives of the business and the courses that people attended.

'The learning that the students were asked to apply in post-module work could be related to improvements in the business. We had developed a methodology which took business needs and broke them down in a generic way, so that we could restate them. These were not competency frameworks – they were just motherhood statements. But there was no way of bringing these things together in the business. People come to work to be professional, and it's the professional side that we needed to cover.'

Reynolds and his team coined a term for what they wanted to achieve: functionality. 'That's an engineering term; it means how you do things very well. The idea was to get away from "competence", because that was hackneyed. Then we asked ourselves, "How do we get functionality?" We created a form of language so that a line manager could talk to me about what he wanted from his people, and I could translate that to communicate what that person needed in his role. Ten or fifteen statements, of one sentence each, were normally adequate. When we had done that, we asked what was needed in terms of knowledge, skills and behaviour. Then we looked at the gap between where we were and where we wanted to be.

'The mistake with the old style was to look first at the gap between present reality and objective, and then to try to work out what skills were needed to bridge it. With the new approach, knowing where we were aiming for in terms of functionality, we were able to target specific shortfalls in knowledge and skills. We still did process and module work, but what we said was: "Let's practise the skills that will matter to people in order to fulfil their roles. Let's not evaluate in terms of knowledge and skills in the abstract, but against functionality."'

With its emphasis on relevance and empiricism, this was a logical development of the WMG approach. Taking it on board neverthe-less stretched even the Warwick staff. 'This was classic stuff in terms of how a company would approach an operational task, but it had never been done in education,' said Reynolds. 'It was fairly revolutionary. It meant that academics had to climb out of their trees a bit, because however lovely the stuff that they were teaching, it really depended on how well people did their job.' It also necessitated a change of attitude by WMG's corporate clients. 'For the companies, it meant that we were no longer just designing the courses. We were also helping their people directly, consis-tently and in greater depth, and this was something they were very bad at,' Reynolds said.

The new model was completed and ready for action by 1996. For WMG, this was not so much a change of direction as a quantum leap forward from the springboard established during its fifteen years of operation. To the gratification of Reynolds and Bhattacharyya, the response from the market was instantaneous.

'Two things happened,' recalled Reynolds. 'First, we started getting enquiries that fitted in with my guess of what companies wanted. Zeneca said: "All our manufacturing people must be more professional." British Aerospace wanted to raise the quality of its purchasing people across the whole group. Then it followed up and said: "All our production managers need to go up a notch." Rover decided that all its power train engineers should go back to school.' In each case, WMG was only one of several universities to be approached and considered by the companies concerned. But the second thing that occurred was remarkable. Reynolds said: 'We won all those contracts because we told the companies that we thought we knew how to fulfil their objectives, how to develop people within their roles better.'

This was no transitory success: the companies concerned, and many more, remained customers of WMG for years. Today, the names have changed, but AstraZeneca, now one of the world's largest pharmaceutical companies, and BAE Systems, the world's second largest defence systems group, still use Warwick extensively. Bhattacharyya's twenty-year link with Rover, which had endured through two decades of ownership by, successively, the British government, BAE and BMW, was broken in 2000, when John Towers' Phoenix consortium took control of the car business. Towers renamed the business MG Rover, and sought advice from Garel Rhys, head of the motor industry unit at the University of Cardiff. But Towers found it impossible to escape the Bhattacharyya influence: for his managing director, he hired Kevin Howe, a former Rover and Rolls-Royce executive – and a very capable graduate of Bhattacharyya's IGDS.

In any event, the Warwick–Rover connection was soon restored. In late 2001, barely a year after Ford bought Land Rover from BMW for £1.8 billion, Wolfgang Reitzle, chairman of Ford's Premier Auto Group, comprising the up-market brands Aston Martin, Jaguar, Land Rover, Lincoln and Volvo, signed a development deal with WMG. Bhattacharyya and Reitzle, the brilliant former engineering and marketing director of BMW, had known and respected each other for years. The relationship had endured despite Bhattacharyya's equally close contact with Reitzle's arch-rival at BMW, Bernd Pischetsrieder, which continued after Pischetsrieder joined Volkswagen. Reitzle recognised that his chances of making Land Rover the undisputed world-leading four-by-four brand − and of creating an integrated and unified group from the variegated Premier brands − could be immeasurably enhanced by working with Warwick. For Bhattacharyya, the Land Rover element was particularly satisfying after the years of work that had helped to take the Solihull business to the point where Ford, the largest four-by-four vehicle-maker in the world, snapped it up.

The Rover empire might have been scattered to different parts of the compass, but Bhattacharyya's legacy also lived on at Cowley, the one Rover vehicle-making plant retained by BMW after it broke up the group. In mid-2001, the renamed Oxford facility began turning out the new Mini − or MINI, as BMW styled the car that it was reinventing as a brand. The event was significant in many respects, but one of them was the implicit tribute to the foundations laid at Cowley in the late 1980s by Barr and Bhattacharyya. Together, they ushered the plant into a new era of manufacturing quality, a fact that was recognised first by Honda and then by BMW as it ploughed hundreds of millions of pounds of investment into the factory.

To those in the know, BMW's continued presence at Cowley was also a reminder of the behind-the-scenes role played by Bhattacharyya in the extraordinary BMW−Rover saga. It was at Warwick, through the manufacturing policy unit that had been established there by Barr and Bhattacharyya, that Rover executives and a team led by Bhattacharyya had mapped out the alternative scenarios facing the business once it became clear in the early nineties that BAE intended to sell out. For more than a year, in 1992–3, in conditions of the utmost secrecy, this team worked through the options facing Rover, from splitting Land Rover ownership from the cars business – quickly ruled out – to examining which would be the most suitable parent for the group.

The list came down to two companies: Daimler-Benz and BMW. Of the two, BMW was seen as the ideal candidate: it lacked any kind of four-wheel-drive product, and it had been the model for Rover's attempt under Sir Graham Day to migrate the brand from the volume to the premium category. The Rover–WMG team were therefore gratified when BMW, of its own volition, emerged as a bidder for the company. The debate about what made the Rover deal disastrous – whether it was the strategy itself or the mistaken implementation of that strategy – will run for years. Bhattacharyya's own view is that the strategy could have worked, but that BMW's fundamental error was to keep the two operations separate. He believes that, had BMW unified the operations – both in manufacturing terms, by making BMW-badged cars in Rover plants, and in management terms, by installing executives from Munich in the Rover businesses – enough design, engineering and production DNA would have been transferred from Munich to make the grand design work. Instead, the operations were kept discrete until far too late in the day.

There is one particular reason why BMW's failure with Rover remains a subject close to Bhattacharyya's heart. The man who facilitated the deal, first by stimulating BMW's interest and then by reconciling the British government to the acquisition, was Bhatta-charyya himself. The trickiest task by far was that of selling the deal to the government. The Department of Trade and Industry, as Bhattacharyya knew very well, had two long-standing loyalties: to Ford, which the DTI had embraced because of its huge influence, as the runaway UK market leader, on employment in the components industry; and to the Japanese 'transplant' owners – Nissan, Honda and Toyota – whose investment in the UK was seen as having provided an international stamp of approval for Britain's car-manufacturing resurrection.

Neither of these two constituencies was going to welcome the BMW acquisition of Rover. Ford wanted nothing more than to see Rover exit the market as a serious contender, whereas a BMW-backed Rover might bring the British company back from the point of no return which it appeared to have reached. As for the Japanese, both Nissan and Toyota shared Ford's desire to see a competitor fall – while Honda wanted to sustain its successful colonisation of Rover by taking control of the business without having to pay for it. Without BMW, Honda would have increased its stake in Rover to 47.5 per cent but would have installed its own managers to sit on the Rover people's shoulders in every department of the company.

On top of the trade opposition, Bhattacharyya had to contend with the ingrained anti-German sentiment in the DTI and the British Establishment. The historic bias against Germany and in favour of Japan was irrational. It seemed odd that the UK could on one hand welcome Japanese manufacturers with open arms and practically on bended knee, while resenting the huge commitment that was being pledged to the only large-scale British car-maker by BMW. However, that was the reality and Bhattacharyya quietly set out behind the scenes to manage it. He played a notable role in winning round Michael Heseltine, self-styled President of the Board of Trade, who did not share the anti-German sentiments, and was largely responsible for giving the DTI a new lease of life and revitalised policy agenda. But Bhattacharyya's efforts did nothing to endear him to others in the corridors of power. Coincidentally or not, while he continued to work closely with Heseltine in areas such as British industrial competitiveness, Bhattacharyya never had the same rapport with the John Major regime as he had with that of Mrs Thatcher.

The reason was clear enough. Like Thatcher, Bhattacharyya was a radical and an iconoclast. He was neither a Conservative nor conservative. There was therefore little to attract him to a government whose leader consciously invoked traditional British attitudes and who emphasised the status quo over the need for change. When Tony Blair was elected leader of the Labour Party, and almost immediately set about jettisoning the discredited legacy of 'them and us' socialism, Bhattacharyya saw a new force for change. The Blairite combination of business-friendliness and multi-racial inclusiveness appealed to him. Like a number of former Thatcher supporters in industry and elsewhere, he welcomed Blair's determination to end the switchback politics of the post-war era by adapting and modifying the new consensus established during the Thatcher years.

Bhattacharyya had dedicated himself to building a bridge between academia and industry; Blair wanted to build a bigger bridge between equality of opportunity and individual incentive. Bhattacharyya felt a natural affinity with New Labour. He demonstrated his support by becoming a trustee of the Institute for Public Policy Research (IPPR), a New Labour think-tank that had certain similarities – in its organisational form rather than its ideological content – with Keith Joseph's Centre for Policy Studies.

Such links with New Labour were forged quietly. To the outside world, the extent of Bhattacharyya's support for Blair only became apparent when the April 1997 general election campaign began. On 10 April 1997, Blair launched his business manifesto – and his appeal for the votes of British industrialists – at Bhattacharyya's International Manufacturing Centre. The visit was intended to emphasise Blair's global perspective as well as his ground-breaking support for the UK private sector. Bhattacharyya and his team had organised a satellite link to their Hong Kong affiliate, where an audience of industrialists had also been assembled. Bhattacharyya made little attempt to conceal his political sympathies. He insisted that he remained impartial: 'We academics will advise anyone who seeks our advice. I talk to all politicians.' He then introduced Blair to the Hong Kong audience as 'our next leader'. Blair was almost equally effusive, echoing the Bhattacharyya mantra of business development: 'Warwick is at the cutting edge of what has to happen for the future,' he said. 'Companies that are doing well are the ones that are making the most of the talents of their people. Countries like ourselves have got to continually move up the value-added chain. We have got to make sure that we are going to compete on the basis of quality with a highly educated and skilled workforce operating the latest technologies.'

Four years on, when Blair returned to the IMC at the start of another election campaign, the links that Bhattacharyya had established with New Labour had been thoroughly cemented. The Professor had advised the Cabinet Office, the DTI and the Office of Science and Technology. He had worked happily with successive DTI secretaries of state, notably Margaret Beckett, Stephen Byers and Patricia Hewitt, counselling them on issues ranging from the future of manufacturing in Britain and e-business to specific situations including BMW's break-up and sale of the Rover group and applications by Rolls-Royce for aero-engine development aid. In spite of Bhattacharyya's close ties to Labour, it was, however from the outgoing Conservatives that he received official recognition for his achievements: in the January 1997 honours, he was awarded the CBE for services to industry and technology.

In parallel, Bhattacharyya's organisation had continued to grow in scale and scope. By early 2001, WMG had more than 474 staff, 1,200 postgraduate and 150 doctoral students, and was training more than 5,000 managers through its international network. It had total income of more than £81m, of which only £1.8m was government-funded. WMG could legitimately claim that its size and self-sufficiency made it unique within the British — and European — academic worlds.

WMG's teaching had improved the competitiveness of companies large and small, in the UK and overseas. They ranged from AstraZeneca and BAE Systems to India's giant Tata Industries,

South Africa's electricity utility Eskom – and H. Burbidge, a 135-year-old Coventry-based family firm whose efficiency in making kitchen doors was transformed in the late 1990s by supply chain management techniques inculcated by Warwick staff. So powerful was the WMG advice that Burbidge was able to grow its market share in Britain and develop an export business from scratch, all this in the teeth of the sky-high pound.

David Burbidge, scion of the firm's founder, gave Warwick full credit: 'At first, I was sceptical about what the Warwick people could bring us, although some of my team were enthusiastic from the outset,' he recalled. 'But I can't speak too highly of WMG. Generally, industry and academia don't really understand each other very well. With Warwick, that is obviously not the case.' Burbidge was sufficiently impressed with the WMG approach that he agreed to lecture on an MSc programme at Warwick custom-designed for top managers in small and medium-sized businesses.

When Blair took the stage at the IMC that day in May 2001, he knew that his vote of confidence in Warwick four years earlier had been justified. He portrayed it now as a pathfinder for university–industry partnership. 'There is now far greater fertilisation between business and the academic world,' he said. 'I am amazed when I go around the country at how many academics are setting up in business. If we live in a knowledge economy, then the creativity that people exercise will be the key to our future wealth.'

The occasion demonstrated a remarkable synergy between the politician and the academic-entrepreneur. Inside the IMC, Blair looked forward to a second term. Outside the centre stood a reminder of how Bhattacharyya was planning to stay ahead in the university–industry game. Atop some seriously high scaffolding, builders were putting the finishing touches to the second phase of the IMC development. As the red-and-white election posters plastered round the IMC walls declaimed: 'The Work Goes On.'

Chapter Four
Taking Wing: BAE, Airbus and Rolls-Royce

During the first twenty years that Kumar Bhattacharyya was active at Warwick, successive British manufacturing sectors were colonised by overseas companies.

The car industry was the biggest single example – not just the vehicle makers themselves, from Rover to Rolls-Royce – but the component companies. Turner & Newall and Lucas Industries were both taken over by American firms; the vehicle systems and parts operations of BBA and TI were sold off; smaller companies such as Adwest and Britax gave up the unequal struggle. Only GKN, with which Bhattacharyya worked occasionally, held on.

Similar retreats from manufacturing empires were logged in a succession of industries, from chemicals and textiles to food and consumer electronics.

But one sector has, so far at least, defied the lengthening odds against British engineering and manufacturing independence. In the early twenty-first century, the country's aerospace industry remained in predominantly British hands. At its forefront were two companies, BAE Systems and Rolls-Royce, whose continued technological competitiveness gave the title national champion a good name. Warwick Manufacturing Group helped both to stay in what industry aficionados like to call 'the sporty game' of aircraft manufacture.

Rolls-Royce was Bhattacharyya's first major customer outside the motor industry. In the mid-1980s, the aero-engine group co-sponsored with Rover the Advanced Technology Centre at Warwick. That partnership paved the way for significant cross-fertilisation between the company and WMG, with Rolls sending engineers to the centre and on IGDS courses.

Although the number of Rolls people involved with Warwick over the years was substantial, the relationship was essentially personal rather than corporate. On the WMG side, the key individuals were Bhattacharyya himself and Trevor Broughton, a former manufacturing and engineering director of Rolls who joined Warwick in the late 1980s and became the linchpin of WMG's ultimately extensive involvement in the UK aerospace industry. At Rolls, the prime movers were Phil Ruffels, who succeeded Broughton as engineering director, and John Ferrie, who headed Rolls' civil engines division and later moved to run the aerospace arm of Smiths Group in 2000.

The collaboration embraced both streams of WMG's activities. Bhattacharyya/Broughton and Ruffels focused on technology development. Their relationship was a long one – it lasted for a decade, until Ruffels' retirement at the end of October 2001. For most of that time, the contacts were unofficial – Rolls had no contractual agreement with WMG, but Ruffels consulted closely and regularly with Bhattacharyya and Broughton. The partnership's informality belied its significance. While Ruffels oversaw a series of engine developments during his tenure, by far his most important and sustained work was on the conception and realisation of the Trent engine family.

It is no exaggeration to state that Rolls-Royce's entire future depended on the success of the Trent. The engine was as critical to Rolls' long-cherished ambitions to become a world leader as the RB211 engine had been twenty years earlier. If the Trent programme failed, Rolls faced oblivion in the big engine market. It would have had no product to offer for the large passenger jets – the Boeing 747 and 777, and the Airbus A330 and A340 – that constituted for the aero-engine companies the highest-growth and most technologically demanding segment of the market. In that dismal event, Rolls would have been relegated to the lowly status of an also-ran behind its American arch-rivals, General Electric and Pratt & Whitney, part of United Technologies Corporation.

As the rollercoaster history of the RB211 demonstrated – the engine both caused the 1971 bankruptcy and nationalisation of Rolls-Royce, and powered its eventual recovery – it was not enough for the Trent to exist: the engine had to work, and work supremely well. If Ruffels, his chief executive (and later chairman) Sir Ralph Robins and their colleagues had any doubt about that absolute imperative, its veracity was hammered home in October 1991. While the eyes of the world were fixed on Moscow, where Soviet Union hardliners were attempting a coup against the reformist Mikhail Gorbachev, British Airways' chairman Lord King announced that the airline was ditching its long-time policy of buying all big engines from Rolls-Royce. Instead of ordering the Trent, BA chose to equip its new fleet of Boeing 777 long-range twinjets with General Electric's GE90 powerplant.

This was a devastating blow for Rolls, which had expected BA to be the launch customer for the Trent. The decision by the national flag-carrier, by far the largest of its relatively few customers, was a massive vote of no-confidence in the engine. The ramifications of the decision seemed to permeate the company: the day that King made the announcement, even the switchboard operator at Rolls' headquarters in Buckingham Gate, close to Buckingham Palace, seemed down in the dumps. Only Robins retained his habitual sang-froid, at least publicly: 'It is a disappointment, but there will be other orders,' he said.

Privately, Robins was less sanguine. He and his team knew that they had to secure a launch customer for the Trent within three months or the costs of staying in the big engine competition would become prohibitive. Frank Turner, Rolls' head of civil engines, was given the assignment. He met the deadline by a whisker, clinching an order from Thai Airways. He followed it with an order from Emirates, the United Arab Emirates airline, and one from Cathay Pacific. That gave Rolls a handhold on the mountain it was trying to climb, but it was only clinging on by its fingertips.

For Ruffels and his engineers, this was only base camp. Having an engine available for marketing was one thing; bringing it to market was quite another. Rolls had now signed contractual obligations to deliver the Trent to its customers by a certain time, at a fixed price, with guaranteed levels of performance in terms of power rating, fuel economy and overall operating costs. It was Rolls' inability to meet its price-time-performance undertakings on the RB211 that had sunk the company in 1971. The Trent's destiny, and that of its maker, now lay in Ruffels' hands.

More than most outsiders, Bhattacharyya and Broughton appreci-ated the importance of the programme and the extent of the challenge. To Bhattacharyya, Rolls-Royce was everything most of Britain's engineering industry had long since ceased to be. Rolls was one of the bare handful of British manufacturers that retained sufficient intellectual property to compete technologically with the best in the world. The Trent was the epitome of what the WMG chief called a 'super-value' product – the kind of leading-edge, high-value product that could create around it a kind of technological cluster, sustaining and enhancing a whole supply chain. Super-value products, of which Britain had nowhere near enough, were engines of economic growth – in the case of the Trent, literally so.

Ruffels never 'employed' WMG to work on the Trent development, but he used Bhattacharyya and Broughton as sounding-boards and sources of advice – while many of his people brought to their work the benefits of what they had learned during spells at Warwick. The upshot was that WMG played a part – a supporting but sustained part – in helping the Rolls engineering supremo take the Trent from Cad screen to aircraft wing. Physically and financially, the effort strained Rolls to the limit. To this day, the company has never revealed the cost of the original Trent programme – the closest Robins came was to remark on one occasion that with such an engine programme, 'you don't get much change out of $1 billion'. In fact, the Trent cost almost double that figure – around £1.2 billion, according to senior Rolls-Royce personnel.

But, thanks to Ruffels' team, that huge investment paid off. Not only did Rolls deliver the Trent on time, it established the engine as the segment leader. So robust was the Trent's design that Rolls was able to use it as the cornerstone of a whole family of engines, from the original 900 to the smaller 500. The Trent enabled Rolls to become, at last, a significant supplier to Airbus aircraft – upsetting the dominance achieved by GE and its ally, France's Snecma. Ruffels' final triumph came in early 2001, when the Trent was selected by almost all the first wave of customers for Airbus's A380 super-jumbo, the largest aircraft ever built.

WMG's more formal work with Rolls was effected through John Ferrie, who instituted a change management programme in the civil aero operations in 1992, and enlisted WMG's help to implement it. Ferrie had first run across WMG when he was running Rolls' marine engines division in Coventry in the eighties. When he launched his business process re-engineering drive in the civil division, Ferrie asked Bhattacharyya to provide the external, academic back-up for the work that was going on at the company's main site in Derby and its component plants elsewhere. 'We took almost a permanent booking with WMG for years,' Ferrie recalled. In total, about 200 of the senior management team attended week-long management programmes at Warwick.

Ferrie's involvement with WMG became much more individual and long-lasting. The change programme coincided with WMG's launch of its engineering doctorate course, and Bhattacharyya prevailed on Ferrie to become a founder student. Because of his career commitments, it eventually took Ferrie six years to complete the – nominally – four-year doctorate. He graduated in 1998, by which time he had established a close relationship with Bhattacharyya, who acted as his personal tutor.

'The experience was very rewarding for me,' Ferrie recalled. 'It was the intellectual challenge and the stimulus to learn. To start with, you would have all these instinctive reactions to situations. You learned to be intellectually rigorous in establishing the foundations for your decisions, the reasons for what you were doing, and being ready to think outside the box.

'One of the great things about Kumar and Warwick is that what they teach is not theoretical. It's practical, it's based on a lot of practical work that he and his group do with their various client companies. So there is a tremendous foundation there of experience. While you might get into a theoretical debate at times, there is plenty of stuff to draw on to validate what you are doing.'

Ferrie, a forthright Scot, was already in his forties when he began studying at Warwick. He had considerable management experience under his belt. He had also 'read a lot of theories and that kind of stuff'. He was, however, well aware that something was missing: 'You didn't get an intellectually rigorous challenge in the day-to-day workplace because you had to move too fast. You had no time to freeze what you were doing to compare it with the theory.'

Ferrie thrived on the cut-and-thrust of the Bhattacharyya style: 'You are always kicking ideas around, discussing economic, management and behavioural models, testing the veracity of your arguments against Kumar. He is a very provocative individual, so when you get into a debate with him, you are never quite sure where he is coming from. He's very adept at throwing out a question and really causing you to think hard. If there's any weakness in your argument, it tends to get exposed pretty quickly.'

The exposure to WMG left an indelible mark on Ferrie's attitude to management. 'The great thing about Warwick was that you came through the programme and out the other end and found that your thought processes had been altered fundamentally. The programme made such an impression that you couldn't even remember the processes you went through before.' That experience informed his decision-making both at Rolls and, later, at Smiths. 'I will go back to Kumar from time to time and say, "Here's my thinking on such-and-such an issue" and bounce ideas off him, get them checked out. That's something I would never have done before taking the doctorate. I am much more willing to have my thought processes examined.'

Ferrie's methodology transfer, as much as Ruffels' quiet conversations with Bhattacharyya and Broughton, highlighted the personal nature of the WMG–Rolls-Royce connection. However, in early 2000 the two parties formalised their links by establishing a teaching company to focus on the integration of engineering design and manufacture in fan systems. 'It's all about reducing lead times,' said Broughton. 'Using research tools, we want to shorten them by 25 per cent. The teaching company will put that into place, and then look for at least another 25 per cent improvement.'

The agreement meant that the Warwick-Rolls relationship was at last taking on the attributes long-established by Warwick and BAE Systems. Here, personal relationships were equally important, but in BAE's case they led to a fully fledged corporate partnership that encompassed many parts of the aerospace giant's operations. As a result, WMG executives and staff played significant supporting roles in two of the biggest industrial stories in recent years: the remarkable recovery of BAE from near-collapse in 1991–2 to leading-edge manufacturer ten years later, and the parallel rise to market pre-eminence of Airbus, the European aircraft consortium in which BAE held a 20 per cent stake.

BAE was a natural partner for Warwick. Throughout the company's tribulations and triumphs, it retained a belief that relevant development of its people would improve the competitiveness of the group. 'BAE is one of the few organisations that has maintained its commitment to developing its people over the decades,' said Tim Bridgeman, Director of Programmes. Just as WMG's approach to clients became increasingly targeted and sophisticated, so BAE's commitment evolved from a somewhat generalised support for individual further education to a more formal, dynamic drive for skills enhancement in specific areas of operation. The vaguely altruistic view that personal development was a good thing gave way to a utilitarian conviction that it constituted a key source of competitive advantage.

This dramatic change in emphasis reflected BAE's corporate odyssey. In the mid-1980s, when its involvement with Warwick began, the company – created by Labour's nationalisation of the aircraft industry in 1977–8 – was barely out of short trousers. It was a single corporate entity in little more than name and management structure. Culturally, it remained a fragmented collection of famous aviation names – Avro, Hawker, de Havilland, Vickers, and so on – that were still fighting battles for independence long after the war had been lost.

A succession of BAE graduate engineers enrolled on the Warwick IGDS and duly obtained their MSc in engineering business management. Others took diploma programmes. Along with Warwick, BAE also used Cranfield Institute of Technology and Salford University. 'We would either select people, or people would select themselves,' recalled Chris Wilkinson, who became head of manufacturing engineering at BAE's Airbus arm in the late 1990s. 'It was all driven by the individual more than the company.' To BAE's mind, the company's encouragement achieved its objective: 'People would get their qualification, feel indebted to the company and their personal contribution would be enhanced.' But the feeling of gratitude quickly passed, and then the company started to see recently qualified postgraduates handing in their notice.

In the later 1980s, under the leadership of Professor Sir Roland Smith, chairman, and Admiral Sir Raymond Lygo, chief executive, BAE assumed the appearance of a unified company. Smith and Lygo could see that BAE was chronically undercapitalised for the aircraft business – both commercial aerospace, where privately funded R&D was unavoidable, and military, where export customers could only be secured if BAE financed large bonds for payment against delivery.

Smith and Lygo pursued a two-pronged strategy to beef up the group's balance sheet. They migrated manufacturing from the historic factories in southern England – Hatfield, Kingston – to plants in the north, releasing the southern prime sites for property development that would generate cash and enhance asset values. That was a lucid and highly effective, albeit painful, unified approach.

Smith and Lygo's other strategic thrust, however, led to disaster. They embarked on a diversification spree designed to buy assets and buttress the balance sheet. Royal Ordnance, the state-owned munitions maker, was one acquisition; Rover was by far the largest. One effect of this approach was to delay the integration of the core aerospace activities by superimposing on them a slate of companies in different businesses. Superficially, BAE appeared to be a unified, coherent group. In reality, it was nothing of the sort. The expansionist effort distracted its management from dealing with the most important core issues, with near-fatal results for the company and, in the case of Smith, terminal repercussions.

As is usual with corporate leviathans, it took a crisis to trigger dramatic cultural change. The 1990 recession blew the diversification strategy apart, causing a cash flow crunch as a multi-billion-pound black hole opened up in BAE's regional aircraft leasing book. Smith was ousted, and for more than a year, BAE tottered on the brink of financial failure. It was saved by considerable good luck and the combined efforts of Dick (later Sir Richard) Evans, chief executive, and Richard Lapthorne, finance director, along with their investment bank adviser, Tim Shacklock of Kleinwort Benson.

They eventually managed to ring-fence the regional aircraft leasing book while raising cash and cutting debt by reversing the Smith–Lygo diversification. The disposals drive culminated in January 1994, when Rover was sold to BMW for £820m. Lapthorne reckoned the deal was worth £1.7 billion when its impact on debt reduction and cash-flow promotion was included. BAE's share price, which had touched 98p at its nadir during the financial crisis, soared and never looked back. It exceeded £20 in the late nineties before settling back at just below £15 towards the end of 2001.

The BAE that emerged from the trauma of the early nineties was very different from the company that had entered that extraordinarily testing time. For one thing, it was a much more solid, single entity. During the survival and revival process, a kind of reunification – or a belated unification – had taken place. Whatever was done, in the field of further education as elsewhere, would now be done for holistic rather than piecemeal reasons. It would also be implemented with a much closer eye on the benefits that it would confer on the company's performance. It would, therefore, be much more targeted and, in the contemporary jargon, output-orientated. There was one other new factor, an ironic one considering that the company had recently jettisoned a chairman who was Professor of Sales and Marketing at the University of Manchester Institute of Science and Technology: new BAE saw management education as an instrument of competitive advantage.

The Smith legacy did contain several positive elements. In particular, the Rover acquisition imported a number of managers – such as Rob Meakin and Land Rover's manufacturing director

Terry Morgan – who went on to take senior posts in BAE. They and other Rover managers also introduced BAE to a different way of approaching manufacturing – the lean, cellular manufacturing techniques whose introduction into Rover had been led by Bhattacharyya.

Initially, BAE executives scorned the notion that the aerospace industry, with its low volumes and craft-based manufacturing and assembly techniques, could learn anything from the high volume, mass-production motor industry. By and large, aeroplanes were put together by hand. But there was a dawning realisation that motor industry techniques were applicable to aircraft assembly. Soon, BAE was breaking down its production lines into cells comprising flexible, multi-skilled operating teams that eliminated traditional demarcation and hierarchical grades. Instead of quality assurance inspectors, the operators carried out self-certification – just as Rover did at Cowley, Longbridge and Solihull. Japanese-style 'kanban' just-in-time delivery systems were also introduced.

BAE's executives had not ventured very far down this path before they realised how much of it was derived from Warwick. 'Rover was well established with our educational programmes when it was bought by BAE. BAE looked at that and said, "We can use this",' Bridgeman recalled. The Warwick people also recognised genuine enthusiasm: 'BAE has a real commitment as an organisation to the development of people,' he added. 'They are one of the few companies to have maintained that commitment over several decades. Their level of commitment is much, much higher than most.'

Many BAE managers did have trouble grasping the extent of the change that was being attempted. Michael James-Moore witnessed a revealing exchange between one BAE man and an executive from Kawasaki Heavy Industries – Kawasaki having been asked by Dick Evans to help educate his people in Japanese manufacturing techniques. 'The KHI guy said they were pretty good at lean manufacturing in their motorcycle business,' recalled James-Moore.

75

'He said they were now planning to apply it to their aerospace business.' The BAE manager asked how long Kawasaki thought it would take them to adopt lean manufacture in aerospace. 'About fifteen years,' said the Japanese. 'You will get about three-quarters of the benefits in five years, but if you really want them to stick, it will take you another ten years after that.' James-Moore smiled at the memory: 'The BAE people all fell off their chairs – they couldn't believe how long the full assimilation process would be.'

Nevertheless, the post-crisis BAE had the will to make a start. The priority accorded to cost-effective education was quickly evident. 'What we saw was a requirement to have a better alignment between the development of their people and what they were trying to deliver within the organisation,' said Bridgeman. 'They put fewer people through our multi-company generic MSc diploma programmes, not only with us but everywhere in the country.' If management education was designed to boost productivity, BAE intended to ensure that the programmes themselves were highly productive.

Historically, BAE had spent around £1m a year on general manufacturing management education programmes with eleven institutions, including Warwick. 'Now we started to get our act together,' said Wilkinson. BAE continued to use a range of institutions, such as Cranfield, for discrete programmes. But WMG was catapulted to the top of the pile.

BAE refined its earlier approach by asking Warwick to pinpoint different subsidiaries – military aircraft, aerostructures, regional aircraft and Royal Ordnance – with dedicated diploma courses. Then, the partnership took a quantum leap forward. A company-wide programme was launched, entitled 'Developing You'. The singling out of the individual within the group was deliberate. BAE recognised that it would get nowhere unless each potential participant bought into the concept. The programme made sense of the hackneyed modernism, Human Resources. It appealed to individual employees to increase the resources of knowledge on which they could draw. The initiative marked a decisive departure from past practice. 'They switched their focus to much more functional, modern programmes,' Bridgeman said. 'That sounds like a lot of jargon, because people say, "Don't you just mean they wanted to promote competence?" The answer to that is yes, but it is competence *within* BAE.'

Instead of focusing on manufacturing education for individual subsidiaries, BAE and WMG adopted a disciplinary approach that crossed company boundaries. The approach aligned education policy with new BAE's emphasis on corporate unity. 'It was driven from the overall values of the organisation,' said Bridgeman. 'You didn't change everyone's behaviour overnight, but the very fact that you were adopting a certain position meant that how you taught the concepts was very different from the previous approach.'

BAE inaugurated a stream of programmes with Warwick: the first, Core Skills in Procurement, was launched in 1997; a second, on Project Management, followed later the same year; in 1998 came Business Winning; in 1999, two new programmes – Manufacturing and Seasoned Practitioner, a title that reflected how quickly much ground had been covered. 'All these were and are driven by functionality,'said Bridgeman. 'They concentrate on what the people in these areas, whatever part of the company they work for, need to deliver – what the business needs from them. This is very different from our historic programme approach. It isn't training – it's education. It is about transferring knowledge with some fairly unique features.'

The procurement programme highlighted the fresh approach. BAE wanted a purpose-designed procurement course that also involved business development elements. The company therefore ignored the Chartered Institute of Marketing, because the CIM ran narrowly defined marketing courses. WMG won the competitive tender for the programme, and followed up by also winning the bidding for the manufacturing programme. The only BAE pro-gramme to be awarded to WMG without a tender was Business

Winning. Warwick's success in open competition highlighted another feature of the group: 'We have always been cost-competitive,' said Bridgeman.

WMG's innovativeness immediately made its mark. With BAE, the group developed a new methodology to ensure that both parties – individual and company – maximised their returns from the programme. First, before each course, Warwick carried out an assessment of each student's individual capability. From that assessment, Warwick drew up a written 'learning agreement', a contract between each participant and BAE. Under the agreement, the individual committed to attain specific goals in return for BAE's investment in his or her self-improvement.

In order to ensure that all the individual's relevant managers bought into the effort, the agreement also contained an undertaking by the individual's line manager to give the student the opportunity to apply the skills learned. The agreement was also sent to a designated senior manager, who would ensure that the line manager honoured the undertaking, and to a manager in BAE's learning and development function. Three months after the end of the course, WMG followed up with an in-company capability assessment.

'It was all about transferring the learning from the programme to the actual company,' said Bridgeman. 'The agreement was really powerful, because from the outset of the contract, it put the emphasis on performance. In each of the individual course modules, people were looking at how to apply what they were learning in the organisation. Post-programme, they had three months to demonstrate that they were performing at the level they were targeting.'

Warwick replicated the learning contract as it spread its wings inside BAE with the ensuing programmes. The contract was and is strictly applied. 'People do fail, and we do use the term Failure rather than Not Yet Competent,' said Bridgeman. 'But the approach is seen by BAE to deliver real benefit.' He cited one instance where participants subsequently saved more than £1m a year as a result of the activity they developed on a procurement course. 'I never claim that educational programmes have direct causal links – you are a fool if you do that,' Bridgeman said. 'But there is no doubt that the individuals involved attribute their performance to having gone through the programme.'

The Business Winning programme highlighted Warwick's ability to harness responsiveness and innovativeness. BAE saw the programme as a cornerstone of its education-based drive to raise its performance. The company told WMG that it needed to win at least £25m in new business every day in order to maintain its order book, while some orders took ten years to win. Unsurprisingly, perhaps, 'BAE was unable to identify any existing educational provider who could supply a programme that covered how you win business in the company's sectors of operation,' said Bridgeman. 'We knew that we had all the right processes and could design a programme to meet their needs. What we lacked was content – we hardly had any that they wanted.'

But WMG knew where to find the subject matter – from BAE itself. 'One of the roles we played was organisation facilitator,' Bridgeman said. 'There is good practice, if not best practice, in almost any subject you care to mention in an organisation the size of BAE. What they can't easily do is organise it, package it and deliver it back to the organisation. We developed a set of processes for working with them, identifying the issues they had to address, then packaging the content that we collected. Of the module that we delivered back to them, quite a small proportion was sourced from WMG. It doesn't frighten us that we aren't a knowledge expert in every subject that we are dealing with, because for us, the processes are the key. We can source knowledge internally, or for that matter, externally, from an appropriate provider.'

The first few Warwick–BAE programmes were under way when the partnership was suddenly presented with a vast new challenge. In late 1998, General Electric Company (GEC), under BAE's former deputy chief executive Lord (George) Simpson, launched

Project Superbowl – a scheme that effectively put its Marconi Electronic Systems defence division up for sale. The move caught BAE by surprise – the company had been in the last throes of negotiating a mega-merger with DaimlerChrysler Aerospace (Dasa). The GEC move threw the Dasa talks into confusion. Although BAE had gone a long way down the road with Dasa, there was no doubting where the priorities of Dick Evans, now BAE chairman, and his team lay. They could see that the future of the defence and aerospace industry lay in electronics and systems – Marconi's core business – rather than in the platforms, the aircraft structures, where BAE was concentrated. Evans had wanted to buy Marconi for years. This was his big chance, and he was not about to lose it.

Just before Christmas, an attempt was made to negotiate a three-way merger of BAE, Dasa and Marconi. It failed, because the Germans insisted that they should merge with BAE first and bring Marconi in later. Evans and co., concerned that Thomson-CSF of France or an American group might buy Marconi, could not wait. They abandoned the Dasa talks, much to the Germans' disgust, and went all-out to buy Marconi. At first, they encountered resistance on this front too. Simpson and his finance director, John Mayo, wanted to merge the whole of GEC with BAE and then demerge GEC's telecommunications arm, forming a new company while leaving the rest with the enlarged BAE.

This was the last thing Evans and his team wanted. They had survived the Smith diversification era by the skin of their teeth and did not intend to exhume the body of the conglomerate from its extremely deep grave. They insisted that BAE would only buy Marconi – nothing else. Simpson and Mayo had little choice but to agree, although they gained compensation for their shareholders by exacting a high price – £7.7 billion in shares – for injecting Marconi into BAE. Agreement was reached early in New Year 1999, although it took almost nine months for the government to approve the merger.

Bhattacharyya had kept in close touch with events, and the WMG executives were among the first to recognise the extent of the integration challenge confronting BAE. The cultures of BAE and Marconi were so different that they were almost diametrically opposed. Marconi's had been learned in the hard school run by Lord Weinstock, Simpson's predecessor as GEC managing director, who had led the company for the best part of four decades. Bridgeman summed up the contrast: 'GEC was very confrontational; the attitude of its management to any competitive or negotiating situation was that it was a case of win or lose – somebody wins, somebody loses. By contrast, BAE's is a win – win philosophy. The lovely feature of that organisation is that they celebrate success. Too many organisations, after a win, say, "Fine, that's done. What's next?" BAE takes the time to give credit where it is due.'

Several pundits believed that the cultural divide was so great that it was unbridgeable – that the merger would go the way of the majority of such deals, and fail to deliver value for shareholders while causing internal chaos. But BAE had other ideas. Evans and his team adopted a radical approach to generate the feeling that this was a genuine merger, not a takeover in all but name, and one that offered opportunities for all retained staff. One novel move was to make everyone in the newly enlarged company reapply for their jobs, in order to establish a sense of equality throughout the group. BAE's education programme – something completely foreign to Marconi – also had a key role to play in ensuring that the enlarged BAE seized the opportunities created by the merger. Discussions were already under way with Warwick about the manufacturing programme. Its scope was now to be extended massively.

Bridgeman said: 'They looked at all the features that we were offering at the time, and the range of programmes that we were running. Then they came to us and said, "We want all these features but with one big difference: we want to involve all our manufacturing people."'

81

That made BAE an order of magnitude greater than anything Warwick had done, including Rover. 'There were 18,000 people in manufacturing in BAE,' said Bridgeman. 'With Marconi, that increased to 35,000. We were not targeting the whole of that population, but with just cell leaders, supervisors and line managers you were talking 5,000 people in old BAE and about double that in the new group. The challenge was clear: how to provide a cost-effective training programme for 10,000 people.'

Bridgeman and his colleagues had to reconcile an apparent contradiction: to produce maximum benefit, the programme had to be relevant to each individual; but BAE could not afford, and WMG could not manage, to be running millions of different courses. The answer the partners devised was to produce a kind of matrix: from the company's side, Warwick designed a specific set of modules that met the functional objectives of BAE: this was called the single development opportunity. At the same time, Warwick and BAE sat down with each participant to identify the highest-priority need for that person against the development opportunity.

'The idea was that everyone should have a personal development plan [PDP],' Bridgeman said. 'If there was an identified development need arising out of the PDP within manufacturing, then manufacturing should develop a new programme – it might be a single module, or half a dozen modules. A lot of the processes here were brand new. They gave us the capacity we needed: rather than have a hundred people doing a set of modules in a year, this structure could accommodate a thousand people. However, manufacturing is the heart of our background, so it was relatively easy for us to get this up and running, despite the scale involved.' In manufacturing parlance, it was mass customisation translated to engineering management education.

Warwick recognised that it could not provide all the modules, so the group prepared to act as prime contractor – another highly appropriate term for the partnership, since BAE's acquisition of

Marconi made it one of the world's leading defence industry prime contractors. To help deliver the programme, WMG envisaged drawing on the expertise of Cranfield, the manufacturing institute at Trafford Park, Manchester, and other organisations. In this respect, the BAE manufacturing programme was a dry run for the transatlantic programme Bhattacharyya subsequently launched with GEC.

Early indications were that the BAE programme would succeed. 'In the first year, 650 different participants made 936 module attendances. With their previous development approach in manufacturing, BAE touched a hundred people in a year at best. So we expanded the amount of "touch" six-fold in the first year,' Bridgeman said. 'And we are in a position to ramp up the volume.'

Managing a huge and sustained increase in demand while simultaneously increasing efficiency and quality was a task that confronted Airbus Industrie in the mid-1990s. The four-nation consortium was structured as a French co-operative, a Société d'Intérêt Économique (SIE) and owned by Aérospatiale of France, Dasa of Germany – both of which held 37.9 per cent of the business – BAE, with 20 per cent and Spain's Casa, with 4.2 per cent. While Airbus was only indirectly accountable to ordinary shareholders – through BAE and Dasa's parent Daimler-Benz – it was only too aware of competitive realities. It had already overtaken McDonnell Douglas, the second American player in civil aircraft, but its long-term aim was to beat Boeing, the industry leader, which at that time held almost two-thirds of the world market.

Boeing's huge volumes, particularly on its 737, the mainstay of most airline fleets, gave it economies of scale that Airbus could not attain until it had expanded its product base to become a full-range supplier of passenger jets. Airbus's first products were the mid-range, wide-bodied A300 and A310, followed by the narrow-bodied 737 rival, the A320. In 1988, Airbus announced development of its first long-range twin- and four-engined aircraft, the

A330 and A340 models. The aircraft, which flew for the first time in the early 1990s, were designed to maximise equipment commonality – sharing components and systems so that scale economies could be achieved.

The largest single common part was the A330/340 wing, designed at BAE's Filton site near Bristol for manufacture at the BAE Chester plant on Deeside, North Wales. Filton and Chester between them had been responsible for every Airbus wing, dating back to the original A300, which entered service in 1974. But this was their toughest assignment yet. Not only were the wings the biggest ever to have gone into production in Britain, but they had to work equally well carrying two very heavy engines – on the A330 – or four somewhat lighter engines for the A340. The designers' solution was a long, narrow wing, similar in shape to that of a glider. This improved the crucial 'lift–drag' ratio which determines fuel consumption levels. The effect of the individual engine weight difference was countered by precise positioning of the outer engines on the A340. However, the parameters in which the designers had to work meant that design for engineering excellence took precedence over design for ease of assembly. This was to cause problems later.

BAE's unique position as Airbus's sole source of wings – a monopoly intermittently challenged by Dasa during Airbus's first thirty years, without success – conferred on the British an importance and an influence that belied their relatively small shareholding in the consortium. Wing production dictates the pace of aircraft manufacturing, for two reasons. One is very simple – a plane cannot get very far off the ground without its wings. The other is less obvious: apart from the avionics, where the French had ensured that they would dominate in Airbus, the wing contains more and higher technology than any other part of an aircraft.

'The body of an airplane hangs on the wing, not vice versa,' Jim Austin, one of Boeing's top manufacturing managers, once observed. '[During production] the other sections are added to the wing. It is kept moving and the rest of the airplane must catch up.' Hence the critical importance of Bristol and Chester to Airbus's operations and ambitions. If BAE could increase wing productivity, that achievement would lift Airbus to within striking distance of Boeing. The consortium could produce more aircraft, faster, at lower cost. Those attributes would offset much of Boeing's inbuilt advantage as the incumbent leader.

So in 1995, with the A330 and A340 in full production, Mike Hodgson, BAE's head of manufacturing engineering for Airbus, set an exacting target for wing productivity. Hodgson wanted to halve assembly time by the year 2000 while cutting assembly costs during that period by 30 per cent. Initially, Airbus Chester made significant progress towards that objective, but then the rate of improvement levelled off. Production volumes on the long-range jets even began to fall. Hodgson's initiative was stalling, and that setback, if sustained, would impact the entire Airbus strategy.

Bhattacharyya, with his ear as ever close to the industrial ground, picked up the opportunity. He contacted Hodgson with a proposal that WMG should work with the Airbus division. To his delight, he found himself pushing at an open door. 'Mike Hodgson was a visionary,' recalled Trevor Broughton. 'Kumar asked him whether he was making these wings in the best possible way, and suggested that he should think about a new way of wing assembly that would deliver the desired efficiency gains.' Hodgson was receptive to the idea. What became known as the Lean Wing partnership between Airbus and Warwick was born.

Bhattacharyya, having forged the link with Hodgson, stepped back for Broughton and Michael James-Moore, the former Lucas manager, to take operational control of the project. The pair embarked on a fact-finding mission, meeting with Hodgson's people, assessing their data and the whole manufacturing process and culture. 'They are quite a macho lot up there in Chester,' noted James-Moore. 'It is essentially a Liverpudlian culture, and they were on piecework, so you had both entrenched, traditional views about how to do things but also a certain instability that comes from a piecework system.'

Hodgson and the Warwick team agreed that the best way to tackle the productivity improvement task was through the framework that had been used by WMG in its early days of industrial partnership. They established a teaching company, under the auspices of the DTI Teaching Company Scheme, in which young graduates called associates, recruited and sponsored by Warwick, would be injected into the Airbus operation to help implement the lean wing programme.

'We wanted to avoid any notion that we were just a bunch of consultants,' said James-Moore. 'Putting consultants in might create ideas, but it very rarely produces anything fundamental because in a situation like this you've got to get under the skin of a manufacturing culture, and be there long enough for something to change. That is very expensive if you do it through the consultancy route. In a teaching company, the associates are working in the company 95 per cent of their time and they have an industrial as well as an academic sponsor. So they are perceived much more as being part of the company, and they are also better able than an occasionally visiting consultant to get a feel of what's acceptable in the company. One of the aims of a teaching company is to allow people to change direction. It takes time for that to happen. '

BAE also bought into the teaching company approach. 'I'm a strong advocate of the Teaching Company Scheme,' said Chris Wilkinson, who succeeded Hodgson at Airbus. 'It is a partnership between government, academia and industry. The emphasis is on learning by doing, which is the win for industry; the win for academia is that the university sponsors these individuals and develops them through its own training courses, while they can also do research with the client. The benefit for UK plc, through the DTI, is that it allows dissemination of knowledge and experience through the industry.'

Lean Wing was launched with Warwick advertising for four

associates to join the Airbus teaching company. In the event, one recruit came from the WMG staff and the other three from answering the ad. They hailed from disparate disciplines: one, a woman, was an industrial archaeologist. The four joined Airbus staff at Chester in analysing the existing operations and helping to formulate what WMG called an 'intellectual direction' for the improvement programme. Broughton and James-Moore spent considerable time at the plant, joining discussions, observing operations and generally acting as coaches to the associates.

One particular defect in the manufacturing process caught their eye: substantial time and effort were required to fit together wing components which had originated in different factories. A detailed plan was drawn up to eliminate waste through a comprehensive review of manufacturing activities. But the plan could not be implemented. It ran into deep-seated problems and became mixed up with several overlapping initiatives. Bruised by the experience, the WMG team members took a step back.

Their rethink reached two important conclusions. First, it was vital that the many and varied Airbus improvement initiatives be prioritised. Accordingly, two associates carried out a detailed survey to fix an order of priorities. Most importantly, Broughton and James-Moore had identified the crux of the productivity problem. They realised that without a more fundamental, strategic approach, Hodgson's efficiency targets would be unattainable.

The next time they visited Chester, Broughton went not to collect facts but to deliver a message to the engineering team. 'I stood up and told them that they did not design for assembly at all,' he recalled. The reaction of his audience was immediate and forthright: 'They wouldn't let us out of the factory. We stayed all day until about seven in the evening and talked to everybody, and a week later they rang me up and said, "You are absolutely right."

'The fundamental issue was that they didn't design adequately for assembly: they designed to maximise performance characteristics,' Broughton explained. 'They aimed to get the last 0.001 per cent efficiency out of the wing, and for the ease of manufacture of individual parts, but not for final assembly.' In other words, the designers had focused so hard on the trees that they had lost sight of the wood. That was why the differently sourced components took so long to assemble; and that was why BAE Airbus had completely to revise its approach to design for production.

A two-day Lean Wing summit, involving WMG staff and senior BAE design, purchasing, manufacture and R&D personnel, was held at Warwick to re-plan the project. All parties knew time was short – by now, the teaching company had only two years left. Experts from Rolls-Royce and the Massachusetts Institute of Technology also attended, to give their advice. As a result, Lean Wing was focused on achieving a 'buildable standard' that would ensure consistent and efficient assembly. The effort covered two main elements: design for assembly and process capability. Broughton sounded the project's new rallying cry: 'No Concessions!'

The project now had two main constituencies: the internal audience at Chester and Filton, and the external audience among BAE's suppliers. In total, 85 per cent of the cost of a completed wing was bought in, so improved supply chain management was essential if the cost reduction goals were to be reached. To address these audiences, a second group of four associates was recruited. They became 'champions' for the construction of demonstrator projects, within the main project, that acted as prototypes for different elements of the changes in manufacturing practice. 'All the way down to manufacturing, particularly in the assembly area, the designers were focused on ensuring that the supply chain could actually deliver what they designed,' said James-Moore. That emphasis had to be redirected so ease of assembly became paramount.

To highlight the problem and what needed to be done about it, the WMG team persuaded BAE to invest £500,000 in a demonstrator cell involving a section of the wing's leading edge. The Warwick team harnessed Statistical Process Control (SPC) and, with an Airbus team from Filton and Chester, started talking SPC with suppliers to establish the current variability of the components they were producing. It rapidly became apparent that, because of the component variability, time to build each wing was fluctuating by up to 100 per cent.

'Part of the teaching company spun off to talk to Airbus's purchasing people,' said James-Moore. 'Inside purchasing, they had manufacturing engineering people as well. Some suppliers had SPC, some didn't. The procurement people didn't think about that – they were lowest-price, not highest-quality. When, encouraged by us, the engineers first went down into purchasing and pushed SPC, they were told they were talking nonsense.But it was one of the levers. I would claim that a lot of the emphasis Airbus purchasing now puts on SPC in the supply chain came as a result of our influence.'

The demonstrator cell enabled the combined WMG–BAE team to zero in on the most important areas of wing assembly. 'A part has dozens of surfaces,' said Broughton. 'But there are only a few that are absolutely key to ease of assembly.' Using the trial cell, 'We demonstrated that with proper dimensioning and consistently accurate tolerances, we could put together this leading edge blindfold,' James-Moore said. 'That made possible a significant reduction in future tooling costs, because a lot less time was needed in setting up the tools for assembly.' So impressed was BAE with the demonstrator technique that it later invested £40m in another demonstrator to redimension the wing for the A320 single-aisle family.

At the end of the three years, there was little doubt that the Lean Wing project had achieved a considerable amount. In precise financial terms, Broughton and James-Moore calculated that it had delivered an improvement for BAE worth more than £2.86m a year on the bottom line. Full implementation would yield an improvement of £5.34m. That was the direct boost to profits; but Lean

Wing also exerted a large but unquantifiable influence on manufacturing practice.

To try to capture more of the efficiency benefits, Hodgson and Wilkinson immediately asked Warwick to start a second project. Four more associates were hired, while six of the first eight joined the Airbus technical staff. Having focused on enhancing the quality and efficiency of manufacturing components for assembly, the successor programme was tailored more towards removing crucial bottlenecks from the assembly process itself. Broughton estimated that up to fifty people were now involved at Chester, together with a raft of designers. 'The areas we were talking about, while they emanated from manufacturing, were things that had to be adopted by engineering,' he said. 'We discussed with the design teams, and got them to accept the sense of what was being said.'

Together, the two projects had significant impact. Most directly, they restored the momentum of Hodgson's productivity drive, and not just on the wide-bodied aircraft. James-Moore reckoned that wing output for the A320 had doubled by early 2000. The 30 per cent cost reduction targeted by Hodgson was partly offset by the huge rise in Airbus volume that accompanied the projects. 'Of the 30 per cent, they have probably got 10 per cent or 12 per cent,' he estimated.

Beyond the statistics, WMG had helped BAE Airbus to improve manufacturing and assembly in numerous ways. 'We introduced them to the concept of Total Productive Maintenance [TPM],' recalled Broughton. 'Then we encouraged them to do more monitoring of their work programmes at different levels within the wing manufacturing process. We developed with them a lot of control systems which gave them better visibility of where they were in the assembly process.'

WMG was too late on the scene to have much influence on the design for assembly of the original A330/340 models. But the lessons of Lean Wing began to make themselves felt when Airbus developed longer-range variants of the A340, the 500 and 600 models. 'The first teaching company undoubtedly influenced the design of the A340-600,' said Broughton. They also made an impact at the deep-seated, cultural level. Broughton and James-Moore concluded: 'Perhaps the most valuable outcome of the projects was that they brought about a return to the days when Engineering spoke to Manufacturing. There is no doubt that lack of communication between the disciplines was a root cause of assembly difficulties.'

Hodgson and Wilkinson rated WMG's contribution highly. 'Trevor Broughton and Michael James-Moore added a lot of value, because they had been in the thick of things in industry and had seen UK manufacturers perform, or not perform,' said Wilkinson. 'Warwick's contribution was not just having these guys stand up and present a module, but to actually be allowed to contribute back into industry. At the end of the day, the degree of success achieved by a teaching company project boils down to personal relationships and whether people are receptive to what the guys were doing. Lean Wing certainly had an effect on me; I learned a lot, and I hope the relationship benefited them as well.'

The project also garnered external plaudits. In 1999, it received an award as Teaching Company of the Year. It also encouraged the Society of British Aerospace Companies (SBAC) to choose Broughton to co-ordinate an industry-wide venture, the Lean Aerospace Initiative (LAI), to promote the adoption of lean production techniques throughout the supply chain. The LAI owed its origins to sources apart from Airbus Lean Wing: one inspiration was a similar American programme; another was the Industry Forum, an initiative launched by the Society of Motor Manufacturers and Traders (SMMT) in the mid-1990s to promote best Japanese manufacturing practice throughout the vehicle component industry in Britain.

The common denominator connecting these various strands was Warwick, which was appointed the lead university on the LAI, working in co-operation with Cranfield, Bath and Nottingham.

Apart from the Airbus Lean Wing projects, Warwick had close links with MIT, which was running the American Lean Aerospace Initiative; as for the Industry Forum, it was run by Graham Broom, a former student of Bhattacharyya's. James-Moore and Mike Hodgson encouraged the SBAC to obtain a £2.5m government grant to fund Industry Forum-type workshops to disseminate the cellular manufacturing message in aerospace. The SBAC went on to train twelve master engineers to lead the implementation of the programme, just as the SMMT had done with the Forum.

Broughton did not underestimate the size of the task in getting lean manufacture ingrained in the UK aerospace industry. 'In the motor industry, you moved from craft to mass to lean manufacture. Here, we are trying to go straight from craft to lean. That is a difficult transition,' he said.

Even BAE, despite thinking about lean manufacture and working with Warwick for more than a decade, has barely scratched the surface. Wilkinson said: 'We started out with Lean Wing talking about how to take waste out of our manufacturing,' he said. 'But "lean" in the broadest sense is about how you do things through the whole business process, from capturing the customer's require-ments with your design to what you must deliver to the marketplace. It goes through the whole supply chain and the whole product life-cycle. It is a mindset issue – you are trying to get people to think differently.'

Both he and James-Moore believed that their joint projects would have made much more progress had they succeeded in capturing total support among the company's top operating management. Instead, James-Moore said: 'It took us the first three years to be accepted on the ground. At the highest level, I'm not sure what we said has been accepted yet. We are, despite everything, still considered outsiders.'

Wilkinson also believed the success of the two Lean Wings was qualified: 'At the level of significant change, there was still a lot more that BAE as a corporation could have got out of the projects.

But we weren't ready. It comes down to sponsorship at the most senior management level. At the time, Airbus was going through a huge growth period. The pace of growth did not allow it fully to embrace the Lean Wing ideas.'

Ironically, given the advantages that it conferred, Wilkinson thought one difficulty was the teaching company umbrella. 'The trouble with "teaching company" is the label; it doesn't create the perception of what is being done,' he said. 'It is a working mechanism that involves people and knowledge share, and certainly knowledge transfer did take place in Airbus from WMG. How that transfer was exploited was a mixed success. These things take time to germinate. Airbus today is getting its head around things that were said three years ago.'

Learning lean manufacture, like the aircraft development process itself, has a long lead time. 'But the people who went through the teaching companies and who were influenced by the guys at Warwick – they have returned to BAE,' Wilkinson said. 'They are much better equipped and as they grow, and rise to more senior positions, they will apply what they have learned and the company will benefit from that.'

Closer to home, in Airbus itself, Wilkinson said: 'There is still a lot more to do. It is difficult to put these lean principles in when your business is increasing by 100 per cent – until you find that you can't deliver what you have committed to: then you look for help. And when you get a new programme, like the A340-500 and 600, some of these principles have been applied.'

But Wilkinson had no doubt that, although some of the Warwick influence rubbed off on the A340 variants, the greatest benefit of Lean Wing would be felt on the programme where Airbus needed it most: the A380 superjumbo.

A380, originally code-named A3XX, was quite an aeroplane – with an initial capacity of 555 passengers, it was going to be the largest commercial aircraft in history. But for Airbus, it was even more than that. The plane gave the Europeans what they had wanted for a long time – an aircraft to beat the original jumbo, Boeing's 747. There was marketing method, not just machismo, in this objective. Since Airbus became a serious contender in the late 1970s, Boeing had always enjoyed an edge because of its monopoly in the jumbo segment. The 747's dominance gave Boeing market flex: it meant that, whatever price-cutting the Americans had to resort to in order to compete with Airbus on smaller aircraft, they could always repair their profit margins because airlines had no alternative to the 747. Or Boeing could play the game the other way – it could cut the price of the 747 in order to entice airlines to buy a package deal including smaller aircraft, thereby closing the door to Airbus.

The A380 promised to eliminate that long-standing advantage. That was why, despite sustained efforts by Boeing to talk down the prospects for an aircraft that large, Airbus executives never wavered in their determination to proceed with the plane. There was only one catch: Airbus had no margin for error. The A380 project was budgeted at $10.7 billion precisely. If that cost rose by more than a fraction, because of development problems or manufacturing difficulties, then Airbus would be in trouble.

Boeing was waiting to pounce: from the moment it became clear in mid-2000 that Airbus would proceed with the aircraft, the Americans let everyone know their estimate of the true cost. Boeing executives predicted with total confidence that the A380 budget would balloon to $17.5 billion. If such an overrun started to occur, Airbus's credibility would be shot. The viability of the aircraft that promised to deliver victory in the Europeans' epic battle for supremacy in the skies would melt like the wings of Icarus, sinking Airbus's lofty hopes.

Airbus won the first phase. Through most of 2001, the A380 project gathered momentum with a following wind of launch orders. In November, after Emirates trebled an original order for seven A380s to twenty-two firm orders, Airbus's chief executive Noel Forgeard forecast that the group would have booked 100 orders for the superjumbo by early 2002. This despite a gathering slowdown in the world civil aircraft market. But the hard work lay ahead. Airbus still had to develop, manufacture and deliver the aircraft on time and to budget. The onus on Filton and Chester had never been greater. If the wing design created assembly problems, the whole project would be in jeopardy.

The two British plants were now under different ownership. At the start of 2001, they had quietly passed out of the hands of BAE and under the banner of EADS, the European Aeronautic, Defence and Space company created by the megamerger of Aérospatiale Matra of France and Dasa, with Casa joining later. Following the creation of EADS, Airbus had abandoned its former co-operative status and become a single corporate entity, 80 per cent owned by EADS with BAE retaining its 20 per cent stake. To quell any fears that the Germans might try to disinvest in the UK, BAE had taken care to ensure that the UK plants were formally designated a centre of excellence for wing manufacture under the new Airbus structure. But there was no doubt that the removal of BAE's protective umbrella made the A380 programme doubly testing for the British operations.

They had already received some more unofficial help from Warwick. Broughton and James-Moore were involved in developing a new manufacturing process for the A380 wing. 'It is different, because of the size and because it is going to be designed with assembly in mind,' said James-Moore. 'That should produce some better ways of fitting it together. Thanks to some US technology, the dimensioning is improved. There will be less swarf [waste]. But it will be a difficult process.'

Wilkinson agreed that 'this is a huge challenge'. But he also saw A380 as an opportunity to deploy, for the first time on a clean Cad/Cam screen, the full lessons of the Lean Wing projects. 'The 380 is the project that will see all the different benefits having to be used,' he said. 'The investment budget is going to be so tight that we are going to be determined to look for every improvement that can be found.

'I truly believe that Warwick's fundamental contribution was to start to get people to think completely differently. On the 380, we will have the chance to do things in a completely different way. I have no doubt that Warwick's contribution to Airbus will be identified and valued more through the 380 than through anything else.' On this essentially confident reading of the future, the superjumbo – the ultimate 'super-value' product – will be the lasting legacy of Warwick's extensive involvement in aerospace.

Chapter Five

The Hobman Projects – Westbury Homes

Eight weeks after customers of Westbury, Britain's fifth largest housebuilder, move into their new homes, they receive a phone call.

The caller, who works for the marketing research firm NOP, asks about the new householders' ownership experience: is everything to their satisfaction? Are there any problems? Four months later – six months after the move – the same process happens and the same questions are put.

This kind of customer after-care is second nature to premium car-makers such as BMW and Mercedes, but before Westbury started the practice, it was completely foreign to the British housebuilding sector, one of the most conservative industries on earth.

The idea, along with a host of other innovations pioneered by

Martin Donohue, Westbury's chief executive, and Robin Davies, its marketing director, was inspired by the long partnership between Westbury and Warwick Manufacturing Group.

The relationship, which has hinged on the close links Davies has forged with Rajat Roy, one of WMG's most senior figures, has been mutually reinforcing. Through Westbury, WMG has been able to apply to a completely different industry the techniques it developed through working with manufacturers. And through WMG, Westbury has been able to flesh out its strategic objective of positioning itself at the leading edge of the housebuilding industry in terms of quality and innovation. The company is widely seen as the most free-thinking of all the big builders.

During the period of the WMG partnership, the Cheltenham-based group has grown from being a mid-sized regional builder making about 2,500 homes a year with annual sales of about £300m, into a genuinely national company that will build around 4,500 homes in its financial year 2000–1.

In the year to 29 February 2000, Westbury increased sales by 14 per cent to £475.9m, raised profits by 26 per cent to £53.6m, and boosted its average selling price by 15 per cent from £80,000 to £95,000 per house. Westbury is quick to acknowledge that its work with WMG has made a significant contribution to that growth.

The seeds of the Westbury–Warwick partnership were sown in the early 1990s, when Davies was logistics director of H. & R. Johnson, a tile-maker in the Staffordshire Potteries. He and Roy collaborated in applying WMG's work on time compression – shrinking the time taken to bring a new product from conception and design to market – to Johnson.

Davies left the firm in 1993 and joined Westbury as group marketing director. It was a big change: 'I moved from manufacturing into housebuilding, which has a completely different culture,' he said. He waited until he had got his feet under the table, and in late 1994 called his old contact at Warwick. 'I knew nothing about the housebuilding industry, except that I lived in a house,' Roy recalled.

The two men had a chat, and agreed that the industry in which Davies was now working had huge scope for improving its entire modus operandi, from the way it built houses to its sales and marketing techniques. The rewards for a company that successfully pioneered such improvements could be substantial. Apart from anything else, there was a great deal of scope to cut the time taken to build a house.

'There was huge potential for process improvement,' Davies said. 'We both said how much the industry could learn from the manufacturing sector.' He asked Roy if WMG, which focused – as its name reflected – on manufacturing – would be interested in getting involved with a different sector.

Roy was intrigued: 'It wasn't just to do with the building process, although that was an important part of our discussion. It was also the first time that probably any housebuilder had thought about marketing as a concept, as opposed to selling.' He and Davies discussed the idea with Bhattacharyya, who agreed that they should explore the possibilities. At that stage, Westbury had not considered moving to manufactured (i.e. prefabricated) houses. But such radical ideas soon emerged.

The newly formed partnership was assisted by a following wind of change. The Department of Trade and Industry – at the time, the sole repository of government work on Britain's industrial competitiveness – had decided to target certain sectors where it believed there was considerable scope for improvement.

The DTI launched a programme called Foresight, which was designed to highlight what the different industries needed to do in order to stay abreast of developments in technology and production techniques and to meet future customer demands.

The government had also been impressed by the Industry Forum, an initiative established under the auspices of the Society of Motor Manufacturers and Traders to improve productivity and quality in the motor components industry, and wanted to start a similar programme in other sectors, including the construction and housebuilding sector.

Anything redolent of the discredited policy of picking winners was of course out of the question. This national effort, albeit prompted by the government, had to be industry-led. Research councils such as the Science and Engineering Council were prodded into action.

They in turn established something called the Innovative Manufacturing Initiative, which was intended to encourage private sector-inspired research into ways of enhancing competitiveness. The initiative targeted four sectors: the motor industry; aerospace; the process industry; and construction and housebuilding.

'This was manna from heaven for us,' said Davies. 'There I was, in a new business in a sector that spent almost nothing on research and development, saying "Can we do some research work?" The next question I was asked was, "What about resources?" Here was a way of starting something off that was relatively low-cost and small-scale, but which could be of considerable importance and relevance to our business.'

'The theme of the sectoral programme was construction as a manufacturing process,' said Roy. 'So we said, "This seems to be a very good vehicle for what we want to do."'

WMG and Westbury jointly applied for a grant towards what they called the Hobman Project. Hobman was an acronym for Home Building as a Manufacturing Process. So novel was such an exercise in the building industry that the project had to start from scratch: first, it focused on setting out an agenda for research, before it even started to identify specific recommendations for action.

They got their grant under the manufacturing initiative, and in January 1996 started work on what became Hobman One. It was a two-year project, using two people at WMG full-time. Davies and Roy also brought in a part-time researcher at the University of

Wales in Cardiff for specific work on the architectural aspects of housebuilding.

'The overall objective of the work was to formulate ideas and a picture of what a professionally run, customer-focused housebuilder would look like,' said Davies. 'What that company would need to achieve in terms of satisfying customer requirements from a production and quality point of view, but also from a service and choice perspective.'

Accordingly, one of their first steps was to get a picture of consumer attitudes. A large-scale household survey, which received about 1,400 responses, was carried out by the researchers 'to understand the nature of demand and to show the mismatch between latent demand and what the housebuilders were providing', said Roy.

The gist of the findings confirmed what both Davies and Roy felt: the existing system was much too rigid and unresponsive. 'The idea was to look at the way the industry, not just Westbury, operated. There is a distinction between what people can afford and what they need. As the industry stood, a particular house price meant this many bedrooms in a house,' Roy later explained.

'But a lot of single people might be quite well off, and didn't need the number of bedrooms specified for the price they could afford. They would have liked the space taken by some of those bedrooms for something else. At the other end of the scale, many people with children needed more bedrooms than the standard model, even if they were small bedrooms.'

The rigidity of the product mirrored, and to some extent followed from, the primitive methods of market segmentation. 'The population was segregated in fairly shallow terms,' said Roy. 'We needed to look at it in much more depth. Westbury, for instance, provided two- to six-bedroom houses, but within each category there was not enough differentiation.'

Housebuilding stood revealed as, in many respects, the antithesis of a customer-orientated business. Instead of being consumer-led, it was production-driven: and the production system itself was innately flawed, tending to create waste rather than eliminate it. If lean manufacturing was the key to business success, then housebuilding was badly missing that key.

That was the way the manufacturing sector had been before the 1980s revolution that forced executives to re-evaluate the way they ran their businesses: production push, not customer pull. It was what Rover had looked like before Bhattacharyya and his team, including Roy, had started working inside the company.

When they realised the extent of the problem, some of the most forward-thinking manufacturers – such as British Steel and Rover – had set about scouring the world for better, and best practice. Davies and Roy now followed in their footsteps.

Instead of merely looking across the industry in Britain, they went overseas – something which, in itself, broke new ground for the not-so-splendidly insular housebuilding industry. Like their manufacturing predecessors, they turned to Japan, where prefabrication was the rule rather than the exception.

With Donohue, who had bought into Hobman's objectives, they visited some of the country's biggest housebuilders, including Sekisiui and Toyota – which, apart from being Japan's leading vehicle maker, is also its fifth largest builder.

The Toyota visit in particular highlighted how Hobman was drawing on the first principles established by Bhattacharyya at WMG: he had been inspired by the Toyota Production System (TPS), of which he had direct experience having worked with Toyota in the late 1970s before coming to Britain.

The system, widely regarded as the world's finest production process, was the inspiration for the 'lean manufacturing' initiatives widely taken up in America and Britain during the 1980s and 1990s by the likes of Jack Welch's General Electric combine. It was popularised in the 1990 book by Professors James Womack and Dan Jones, *The Machine That Changed the World* – the machine in question being the TPS.

Davies and Donohue were struck by some of the Japanese factory sights. 'At Toyota, we saw modular volumetric units going down a moving line,' said Davies. 'As it moved down the track, there was a guy fixing tiles inside. There it was, right in front of us: manufactured housing.'

In Britain, 'prefab' had all kinds of down-market connotations after experiments in the seventies and eighties that were, from a customer viewpoint, less than satisfactory. Japan showed prefabrication in a completely different and far more agreeable light, as part of a whole housebuilding process distinguished by high quality and responsiveness to the customer.

'We found the whole process in Japan very, very different,' said Davies. 'The way the customers choose what they want is a very long-drawn-out process involving catalogues and details such as the kind of wood required. It goes to a level of detail that we wouldn't be capable of offering in this country at the moment. The product was distinguished by space and choice as well as the finished quality.'

Not everything in Japan was impressive. 'We saw a lot of what we thought was wastage,' Davies recalled. 'Not every company was lean: you went into some of these factories and you couldn't move for people.' Nor was all of what they saw particularly relevant: 'A lot of these products were over-engineered because they had to cope with earthquakes and so on,' he added.

The tourists also knew that the Japanese system could not be simply transplanted to Britain. 'We didn't say, "Gosh, we must have that for the UK." The houses that we visited would not have much of a market here.'

The translation they made from their Japanese study tour was not literal; it was parallel and generic. Davies said: 'It was a matter of taking the component approach and the attention that goes into the design and assembly process, and saying, "Wouldn't it be great if we could achieve that in the UK in our own products?" Here was a company that was actually making a success of producing a much higher quality product. It was the principle of process improvement – that was the focus of what we brought away.'

Donohue's presence on the trip was crucial, because it meant that from now on, the work of the Westbury–Warwick partnership would have the best boardroom champion imaginable. 'Having Martin Donohue there was very helpful, because he started saying, "There is a different way of doing this."' From that moment, the Westbury revolution was on course.

Davies and Roy already had a good idea of what their objective should be. 'We needed to provide more managed customer choice. You couldn't go for a completely customised house, because the majority of housebuilders in this country are speculative builders. So you needed a concept of mass customisation. We started to look at how that could be addressed.'

It was obvious that, without technological innovation, mass customisation would remain a chimera. 'With current technology, it took at least sixteen weeks to build a house,' said Roy. 'If you were going to customise it, that would just increase the timescale, so you couldn't really do it. Plus, you could get a quality problem – subsidence or whatever.

'Some of that was an organisation issue, but some of it was technology-related because the technology wasn't robust enough to provide right-first-time.' And right-first-time production was a prerequisite for attaining the goal for which Westbury and WMG were aiming.

There were other reasons that made an emphasis on technological change essential if Westbury was to achieve its aims. 'One of the big factors was shortage of skilled labour,' said Roy. 'The family trade was disappearing. Most of the companies had stopped training people – Westbury and its peers only employ office staff and site managers. They don't employ anybody actually working on the site.'

The technology imperative was also highlighted, indirectly, by the Japanese visit. Roy said: 'One of the first things that came out of Hobman One was the realisation that you can't just take a technology and put it into your building process. The problem in Britain is the opposite of Japan.

'Apart from Toyota, the other big Japanese housebuilders were originally steel makers who diversified, plus people who dealt in timber framing. Their vertical integration gave them an outlet for their materials. In Britain, wherever the technology is available, it isn't owned by the builders. They don't have any manufacturing technology whatsoever. So we needed to start to bridge that gap. There was obviously so much room for technological improvement before you specified the product.'

Davies gained a further insight into the innovation process in late 1997, when he spent some time at the University of Washington's business school in Seattle on a Harkness Fellowship, sponsored by the *Financial Times*. 'I was exposed to a range of different IT and high-tech industries and the way that they manage innovation and change,' said Davies.

Hobman One ended in 1998, having mapped out the way ahead for Donohue and Davies. 'The ideas and processes that came out of the work started to assume a central position in the formulation of strategy at Westbury,' said Davies. 'We came out of Hobman One with a sense of how we would like to change Westbury for the future.'

On the technology front, Davies and Roy catalogued all the different ways to build houses, and applied a series of criteria to those approaches, scoring them on a star system. 'We looked at everything,' said Davies. 'Timber-framed; steel-framed; panel-based things; flat-packing; volumetric. As well as Japan, we looked at the US and Europe – there was quite a lot of innovation in Holland, for instance.'

They concluded that no one had a total solution which would match the needs of Westbury's present and potential customers. 'So we started to say, "If we pick the best from these ideas, what would the system look like?"'

They were aware of the problems associated with manufactured housing. Roy said: 'In the past, people had gone for this kind of housing without enough research and development. It wasn't market-driven. The whole concept was prefabrication of standard units, as opposed to providing customer choice. We still have prefab, but now the whole thing is about customer choice.'

Within the building process, the partners concentrated on the method of manufacturing the shell of the house. 'With brick and block, the accepted methods, we were taking seven or eight weeks to do this part of the job,' said Roy. 'We are now talking about getting the outdoor structure up in one to two days using a lot of pre-built and pre-manufactured.'

They had to work through the differences between manufactured technologies. 'Some are quicker than others, some are more amenable to providing greater choice than others,' said Roy. So, to progress what was still essentially an R&D programme, Westbury linked up with various builders to make prototype houses using a particular technology.

They tried steel-framed housing. 'That had quite a lot of scope,' said Davies. 'It brought the precision that we were looking for, because we needed to be able to build a precision backbone for the house that would then enable us to bring in components and snap them into place, rather than need armies of people, who supposedly had these special skills, with saws, hammers and Mastek guns to make these things fit.'

Westbury worked closely with British Steel, which was able to improve its steel-frame manufacturing system as a result. Several prototype steel-framed houses were built and sold by Westbury Developments, the company's R&D arm.

WMG kept a close eye on the prototype work. Davies said: 'The Warwick team became very good at observing the building process, then providing feedback and saying, "Right, this is how you can improve the process and this is where its strengths and weaknesses are."'

Assisted by WMG, Westbury also experimented with panel-based systems using cement particle board injected with polyurethane foam inside the factory. But the system, which had been developed by Marshall's, a building materials firm, was very heavy. Westbury concluded that the product was over-engineered for the consumer market, and also expensive.

Nevertheless, a prototype house was built using the system and was quickly sold. Although the co-operation with Marshall's continued for a while, it was ended by mutual agreement when Marshall's decided to focus on the commercial sector, where it had a ready market.

Westbury then learned of a different panel system invented by Keith Williams, who ran a small Cornish business called Thermatech. 'We shot down to see him,' said Davies. 'He had basically developed what we had imagined and specified from the trials we had run with Marshall's.'

Moreover, Williams used phenolic foam, one of the best fire-resistant materials, widely used in vehicles and fridges because it is an excellent insulator. The foam injection process had posed problems, but Williams solved them by recruiting a young materials scientist from the University of Plymouth who devised a way of injecting the foam into a flat panel.

Williams then patented the process. 'As soon as we saw it, we knew this was exactly what we had in mind,' Davies said. This was the key to practical implementation of the manufactured housing concept Davies and Roy had developed.

The result of all this effort was made known to the world at large in mid-April 2000. Westbury announced it had acquired a derelict double-glazing factory in Castle Bromwich, Birmingham. It was a phoenix-from-the-ashes story, since the company that owned the factory – which had employed 600 people at its peak – had collapsed a year earlier.

Westbury planned to invest £10m in rebuilding the plant, which would be opened in early 2001 as a new business in the Westbury group, called Space4 and run by Robin Davies. The venture immediately attracted headlines about 'assembly-line houses'.

At full capacity, which it would reach within three years, it would be building parts for 5,000 houses a year – more than Westbury's current output. But then, Westbury did not intend the production to be solely for its in-house needs: it planned to sell part of the output to builders in Britain and mainland Europe – furthering Donohue's aim of redefining and broadening the scope of its business.

The factory would produce timber wall frames with insulation injected between an inner plasterboard wall and the outer cement particle-board wall – courtesy of Thermatech. It would also turn out floor units comprising joists and floorboards pre-drilled for pipes and cabling. This would compress housebuilding time because electricians would no longer have to wait for bricklayers to finish the outer wall before going in. It was replacing sequential with simultaneous engineering.

The factory workforce would be 120 people, with another eighty employed to assemble the components on site. Assembly would take one day. As a result of the new system, the total time taken to build a house would be halved from sixteen weeks to eight.

Davies did not focus solely on the speed of construction. He also emphasised the greater precision and quality built into the new system: 'The system is manufactured to a tolerance of less than five millimetres,' he said. 'This means an end to badly fitting components such as kitchen units and, because the process is completely dry, the elimination of cracks caused by shrinkage.'

Space4 did not result directly from the Warwick work on Hobman One, but without that partnership it would not have come into existence. Davies said: 'What Warwick enabled us to do was to identify very clearly the characteristics of the system we were looking for.'

But that was only part of the Westbury–WMG picture. As

Davies acknowledged, other housebuilders were also moving to factory-assembled sub-systems. But where they tended to see such a move in a single dimension, as efficiency-enhancing, Westbury had a multi-dimensional approach.

'This broad-based strategy was one of the big benefits we have derived from our collaboration with Warwick,' Davies said. 'Lots of our competitors are also looking to other construction methods, but they aren't really addressing the cultural issues as rigorously as we believe we are.'

In line with WMG's holistic approach to technology management, Roy advised Davies that Westbury needed to re-engineer its approach across the board if it was to reposition itself successfully. 'We recognised that technology on its own was not enough,' said Roy. 'Around that, we needed to do all sorts of things in the business processes.'

Davies agreed: 'Hobman One was not just a new process that would improve our capability to deliver quality; it was also to do with organisation: what would we need to be able to embrace this technology-orientated approach and these new processes,' he said.

'We saw the biggest challenge as being culture change, not just within Westbury but in the sector as a whole. You can come up with the best processes in the world, but unless you can persuade people that they are the right way to do things, you will never make them stick.'

Hobman One's influence on Westbury culminated in 1997 when Donohue launched Westbury Values, a group-wide culture-change programme, at Birmingham's National Motorcycle Museum. The programme set out the key elements in the company's plan to change the way it did things. 'The majority of our competitors would look at that and wonder what it was all about,' said Davies. 'You could say it was touchy-feely stuff, but it was crucial to provide an internal focus. We wouldn't have done that without Warwick.'

Westbury obtained a technology transfer grant from the DTI to implement some of the ideas spawned by Hobman One. Within the company, it established quality action teams to make increasing quality a continual improvement process – something it had learned from the motor industry, in particular from WMG's Rover work.

A staff retraining programme was started. It combined training with continuous improvement, so that the training side was tailored to focus on the specific area of work for which the individuals concerned were responsible.

The company also raised its sights in recruitment. 'We have now got a graduate programme, which we didn't have before,' said Davies. Westbury company hires twelve graduates a year. 'It is central to our succession plan for the future,' he said.

The most influential graduate came from Warwick. David Craig, one of the products of Bhattacharyya's engineering doctorate programme, was recruited by Davies to provide research that would support implementation of the change programme. Craig's role highlighted WMG's openness to industry. He spent all his time at Westbury while pursuing his Warwick doctoral studies.

'Part of the problem [of implementing change] related to who was going to champion this,' said Davies. 'It has to be done at a very senior level, and if we were to succeed we needed research to help us formulate plans and proposals.'

Research capability also played an integral part in Westbury's interpretation of the extended enterprise. 'In research provision, we saw the opportunity to do the same for our key suppliers, using engineering doctoral students,' said Davies. 'The brick people came to us and said, "We want to get involved". But they asked us what ideas we had.' Westbury and WMG linked with Ceram, the ceramic industry research centre, and placed a doctoral student there.

'The idea was to set up a network of these students which would link with us day-to-day and be a 100 per cent dedicated resource that would work with us on this improvement programme,' Davies said.

In October 1998, the second phase of Westbury's partnership with Warwick was formalised in a programme that Davies and Roy called, naturally, Hobman Two.

'By the time we got there, we had decided to do Space4, so Hobman Two is a very much more focused programme of research,' said Davies. 'It is entirely focused on our new processes.'

These processes cover different aspects of the housebuilding business, ranging over a broad canvas. They involve breaking new ground and setting new standards for the industry in every area covered. They will also feature extensive capitalisation on the opportunities opened up by e-business, of which Davies became aware during his spell in the US.

'It was the start of e-commerce, with Amazon just getting up and running, so it was a very exciting time to be there. I got swept up in the whole dotcom energy of the place.' When he returned, he knew that on the business-to-business side of the company, 'e-commerce comes right in the centre of things'.

Davies deliberately called one of Hobman Two's focal points 'connectivity', a term stolen from the IT industry. 'It is based on the earth-shattering idea of designing components so that the house fits together properly,' he said. 'Housebuilders deliver modules to a muddy field and expect someone to put them together, whereas in other industries people have minimised the raw materials and made components to put together. Why can't you do that with a house?'

Westbury and WMG analysed different joining techniques, including the use of adhesives rather than nails and screws, to provide a better finish. They explored easier ways of installing doors and windows with less obvious fasteners. 'It was about combining greater quality with more speed in the process,' said Roy.

Another important characteristic of the research was the quest for flexibility, or what Davies called 'disconnectivity'. 'People want to change their house after a time,' he said. 'We thought, "Why not design kitchen and bathroom fittings that can be disconnected instantly?" So instead of making your house a building site when you wanted to change it around, it could be more like an Airfix model diagram.'

Accordingly, they investigated modular heating systems. Roy said: 'If you are a single person or a couple without children, then the ideal solution is to start off with a small boiler and add to it as your need changes.' They also did some pilot work on wiring so that it was integrated with the shell of the house, and so that plug points were provided around each room enabling furniture to be moved as the homeowners' circumstances changed.

'The idea was to manage choice, hopefully extending that as we became more familiar with the process. We wanted to provide as much internal customisation as we could,' said Roy.

Hobman Two involved Westbury in another kind of connectivity: with its suppliers. Given its strategy of taking product and service quality to a new level, the commitment to supply chain management was inevitable. However ambitious Westbury's ideas, the company would be unable to bring them to fruition unless it could take major suppliers along with it.

The task of convincing suppliers to adopt the new practices was helped by technological innovation. Because much of the technology Westbury was using was new, so were many of the suppliers. They came without the baggage of history. But more established suppliers also bought into the project. About six participated in Hobman Two. Among them were Stairways, a staircase manufacturer, and H. & R. Johnson, the tile-maker where Davies had first made contact with Roy.

Westbury thus became a classic extended enterprise, and started to reap the benefits from the community of interest and action it was creating. 'We have used the project to establish other types of relationships with suppliers that are nothing to do with negotiating the price,' said Davies. 'So we meet lots of people we wouldn't otherwise meet, in R&D, product development and so on, who have contributed to the project.'

In several aspects of the supply chain management process, Roy drew on WMG's work at Rover. Particularly strong emphasis was placed on creating a team-working ethos, both within Westbury and between Westbury and its suppliers.

Just as Rover had done, Westbury and WMG formed temporary, multi-disciplinary teams to help a supplier fix a specific problem. Elsewhere, increasing emphasis was placed on replacing the traditional tradesman system with team-working. 'Ultimately, there will be a small team to put on the house exterior and then a team for metal work,' said Roy. 'This will be instead of having individual trades come in and do their bit and blame someone else for a problem.

'There will be a process sheet for these teams, not for individual trades. The team will consist of people who aren't necessarily employees of Westbury, but who have been put together by Westbury.' The company was considering going still further in its quest for refining the quality process.

Roy said: 'In the future, it is possible that Westbury might itself employ a finishing team or something like that. It would be dedicated to improving quality, which is needed if you are to customise a house very quickly.'

Another initiative within Hobman Two was the development of a process engineering information system, something which Warwick had helped develop at Rover. 'The big problem in construction and housebuilding is that every builder does what they like,' said Roy. 'The concept of process doesn't exist. There is no standard practice.'

One of Westbury's decisions during the overall change programme had been to move from using lead plumbing to plastic plumbing, because plastic provided more design flexibility. Roy said: 'The usual problem was that the plumber then came along, had never seen plastic plumbing before, found a problem and cut a piece of lead piping and attached it to the plastic piping – thereby defeating the object of the whole exercise.'

So Westbury, with WMG's input, introduced a process sheet that documented the best standard production engineering practice for its suppliers to follow. The idea was inspired by something done by Land Rover, with whom WMG had worked.

At first, the sheet was only a conventional manual. The partners then began developing a computerised version that allowed for customisation: 'Some will be specific to various house types, some to regional variations, some to a specific plot or customer,' said Roy.

'If every house has something different, to remember what those differences are is absolutely fundamental.' The databank will also act as a channel for transferring best practice from one part of Westbury across the whole company, and from the company to its suppliers. 'It will be a communication and feedback medium, a multi-media system,' said Roy.

That was only one aspect of the way in which Westbury was now harnessing information technology to reach its goals. 'We are bringing into play a number of our e-commerce ideas,' said Davies. The company established its own e-procurement hub, initially in a modest way but with what Davies said was 'tremendous scope for enhancing efficiency'.

'The waste in the supply chain was, traditionally, huge. That was brought home to me when I came to Westbury and saw that they measured wastage in double-figure percentages for some raw materials. There was this accepted relationship between quality and price: I was told that there was 12 per cent wastage in some bricks, but that we had only paid "X" for them.'

That reaction was a measure of the mindset revolution that Westbury was trying to achieve. 'It reminded me of the story of the Japanese firm that was asked by a British customer to supply a component with no more than 5 per cent defects,' said Davies. 'They delivered the components in two packages, one large, the other small: the big one contained perfect, defect-free parts; the other had parts with 5 per cent defects.'

That traditional mentality could be eroded by Westbury's emphasis, kicked off through Hobman One, on factory-made sub-systems, where faults were easier to eradicate. 'We have 140 different building sites at the moment, all receiving lorry deliveries of individual bits and pieces for each house,' Davies said in September 2000. Space4 would begin to change all that when it came on stream, but e-procurement would make the whole supply chain leaner.

'We can also at last start to work on cost-engineering,' Davies said. 'There are so many sources of saving on waste. We can say, for example, "If we redesign the house this way, we have only got four lengths of wood to deliver." That brings savings on packaging, savings on number of deliveries, and so on. It speeds up the process and cuts the expense. We can feed the savings back through the supply chain, and share the benefits.'

Westbury's ultimate aim is to compress the whole building chain, from customer order to moving in, to six weeks. 'There's not a lot to gain beyond six weeks, because of the legal processes of buying a house,' said Roy. 'At present, apart from the actual construction taking about sixteen weeks, the companies build speculatively. The process could go as far as not being at all speculative, but purely because of seasonal variations there will be an element of speculation. So you might build the shell but leave the internals to be built to a specific customer order.'

The revolutionising of the build process had its corollary on the sales side, in the relationship between sales person and customer. In Hobman Two, this area is known as 'visualisation', although it might just as well be termed 'virtualisation'.

Davies said: 'We know we are going to end up building these houses very much more rapidly, and that we'll offer more choice. So we've got to find better ways of demonstrating that customisation to the prospective buyer, without having to build one of everything.'

A Warwick researcher is therefore working with Westbury on

building a computer-based interactive system for the customer to access, which will be integrated with Westbury's e-procurement hub. The system will allow the customer to experiment with different house configurations, and it will be able to inform the customer what is and is not possible. 'So as you are sitting in front of the screen choosing the composition of your kitchen, there is a bill of materials building up behind the screen which can be sent through the internet to the relevant suppliers, who are also on line,' Davies said.

Westbury plans to install the system in each sales office, but that may be only an interim step. The company reckons that about 40 per cent of prospective buyers already visit its website; eventually, it would be logical for the interactive design-your-own-home system to be accessible from home through the web.

Such a technological jump would dovetail with Westbury's ideas for transforming the sales process. Davies said: 'The sales office is another issue which we are looking at. Today, you can buy a £1,000 ticket for a round-the-world air trip from your living room. Yet you spend £100,000 or £200,000 on a house and are expected to make your own way into the office where you are buying it. Should we go to people's homes? Or have a high street presence where people could come in and use the computer system?'

It is a safe bet that, with Westbury, this drive to think outside the box will amount to more than pie-in-the-blue-sky theorising. Donohue's dictum is simple, but horizon-expanding: 'We need to be more than just a housebuilder if we are to increase our total return to shareholders,' he said in May 2000.

Accordingly, and entirely in line with the radical changes explored and inspired by the Hobman projects, in early summer 2000 Westbury launched Westbury Direct, a business that will eventually offer house buyers a one-stop shop for buying household fixtures and fittings, from carpets to bathroom equipment, and home-related services.

Westbury Direct's pilot venture relates to white goods –

cookers, fridges, washing machines and the like. Customers can visit a Westbury sales office and obtain a catalogue with a web site address. They can then go home and select which appliances they want in their new house. The system, which has certain affinities with the process of choosing options for a car, enables the customer to buy better products than those offered as standard. The order is fed through to the relevant supplier, with Westbury acting as intermediary.

'That ultimately will develop into an e-business with someone like Hotpoint sitting at a call centre which answers as Westbury but is manned by Hotpoint people,' Roy predicted. 'This is Westbury putting customer and supplier together.' Davies said that part of the purpose of Westbury Direct was 'to ensure that we start the house-buying process face-to-face'. In other words, it is one more detail in the overall Westbury strategy: to build its brand and its relationship with the customer.

The Westbury people believe this is what marks them out from rivals who are focusing at different points in the housebuilding chain. 'There are lots of individual experiments going on, with timber- or steel-framed houses for instance, but they are like taking a needle through a part of the organisation – they can make only a relatively small change.'

By contrast, Westbury's top executives are trying to take everyone – its staff, its suppliers, its customers – along with them across a spectrum that they are redefining and extending. Roy said: 'This is very all-embracing work. They are trying to define a completely new industry.'

Roy sees the Westbury partnership as being, in its own right, an exemplar of best practice in industry–university collaboration. 'This is a classic example of research, technology transfer, and a relationship which allows dialogue with us acting as a catalyst for thinking new things, which they would then pick up on and investigate in more depth.'

The feelings are mutual. Without Warwick, Davies believes,

Westbury could never have come so far, so fast. His view is informed: apart from his American experience, he has worked with a number of Britain's top universities. 'Warwick Manufacturing Group is simply the best at working with industry,' he said.

'Part of the reason for that is that it understands the way industry works. Small things matter in this relationship between industry and academia; the cultural match is so important. With one well-known university, we ended up in an argument about who was going to pay for the photocopying.'

Equally distinctive, he said, is WMG's hands-on attitude. 'There are those universities that, like management consultants, see their role as being an observer and then think they have achieved something when they have reported on it. That has a certain value, but it is nothing like WMG's willingness to roll up their sleeves and take some responsibility for solving the problems. In this respect, I haven't come across another university that comes anywhere near.

'WMG doesn't do anything until it has got an industrial partner. The people there are willing to take a risk with you; they know that nobody in industry at the beginning of a research project wants to chuck cash around. This is very much a trust thing, but it is based on commercial nous. WMG also happens to be world class at what it does.'

Davies became so convinced of WMG's quality that he signed up personally for an engineering doctorate in the implementation of innovation in industry. 'I've got the Warwick bug,' he said. 'But then, it is a very special place.'

Chapter Six

AstraZeneca — Part of the Process

David Barnes and fellow executives of Imperial Chemical Industries were on red alert. It was June 1993, and the pipe-smoking Barnes, an ICI veteran, was poised to lead the group's pharmaceuticals arm, recently renamed Zeneca, into a stock market flotation. The move would transform ICI, the venerable repository of much of Britain's bulk chemical industry, and liberate Zeneca, whose leaders had long pressed for the highly rated drugs business to be demerged into an autonomous public company.

Now the epoch-making day dawned — but a vast shadow overcast the great event. Ever since ICI had first mooted splitting off Zeneca, the business had been stalked by Hoffman La Roche, the Swiss pharmaceuticals giant known — and notorious — in Britain for the marketing of Valium in the 1970s. Roche and its advisers at the ill-fated British investment bank Barings saw Zeneca as a dream takeover prospect. In the huge but highly fragmented international pharmaceuticals industry, the acquisition of Zeneca would catapult

Roche into a powerful position, ranking it alongside the leaders, America's Merck, Britain's GlaxoWellcome and the transatlantic combine SmithKline Beecham.

In a sense, takeover threats were nothing new to Zeneca. The company had been born out of one such threat – the attempt in 1991–2 by Hanson, run by Lords Hanson and White, to pressure ICI into agreeing a takeover bid. Hanson bought a small stake in the group and began a protracted siege which was eventually defeated by a sustained and determined counter-offensive. Internally, the defence included Project Dawn – later retitled Project Mortar – which detailed what became the pharmaceuticals hive-off plan. Hanson removed his tanks from ICI's Millbank lawn in May 1992 and less than three months later, on 29 July 1992, ICI's board voted to demerge the pharmaceuticals business. The name Zeneca was subsequently adopted after an exhaustive trawl through all kinds of possible names, real and manufactured. It set a trend for scientific- or technological-sounding company names, frequently deploying the more rarefied letters of the alphabet in unusual forms.

Having emerged from the Hanson battle, ICI and the Zeneca team had no intention of surrendering to the Swiss. They rebuffed informal approaches by Barings, suggesting that the flotation be scrapped in favour of a trade sale of Zeneca to Roche. Barnes and his new team, including the finance director and former Warburgs financier John Mayo, were adamantly opposed to this, and their trenchant views bolstered the resolve of the ICI board. But the ICI camp knew that the matter was ultimately out of its hands. Roche was big enough to make a hostile bid for the whole of ICI, or – more likely – to pounce on Zeneca the moment it reached the stock market. Roche certainly had the money for such a bid. The real question was whether it had the nerve.

Hostile bids in the pharmaceuticals industry were almost unknown – Merck had never made one, the SmithKline Beecham merger was friendly, and even Glaxo's takeover of Wellcome, although it was against the wishes of the Wellcome board, was only executed thanks to support from the Wellcome Trust, which effectively controlled the company. Moreover, Roche had been scarred in the 1970s by the bad publicity it had received in Britain over its Valium product. The company had worked hard over twenty years to repair its reputation in the important UK drugs market, and executives were worried that an aggressive attempt to gobble up Zeneca, seen as a nascent national champion, would rekindle memories of the old controversy. In Roche's home town of Zurich, the bid plan was put on hold.

Unaware that Roche was bottling out, Barnes and his team approached the red-letter day, 1 June 1993, with a combination of excitement and trepidation. That morning, as Zeneca began trading, the directors watched and waited anxiously for a raid on the shares by the Swiss. Nothing happened. In the ensuing days, as Zeneca shares rose in value, the immediate prospect of a Roche bid faded away.

For several years afterwards, Barnes and co. had to live with the recurrent threat of takeover – if not by Roche, which continued to track Zeneca, then by Glaxo, whose boss Richard Sykes made no secret of his determination to expand through another mega-deal. Every expert agreed that the pharmaceuticals industry must consolidate; most saw Zeneca as a consolidatee, not a consolidator.

This perception seems to have had at least two effects, both of them highly beneficial for the business. First, the view of Zeneca as a perennial bid target caused the share price, the odd blip apart, to rise steadily. This created a classic self-denying City prophecy: the more speculation there was, the higher the price went – and the less likely it was that someone would actually bid. Roche, for instance, looked several times more – each time reckoning that the price was too high, only to see it rise further. Finally, when Zeneca shares went past £20, the Swiss turned their backs on the company for good.

The second effect was to make Zeneca's top management try

even harder. A newly created company, particularly one of Zeneca's size and potential, is not short of motivation. But the awareness that one stumble could create an opportunity for a predator kept every executive on their toes. Together, this combination of freshness and latent threat created an incentive for the Zeneca team to look at business issues differently and in greater depth than a more established, less motivated management might have done. Zeneca was smaller than many of its peers, but it could also be smarter and more nimble. Barnes created a climate in which his colleagues were encouraged to question received wisdom and to seek new ways of finding a competitive edge. One of the areas on which Zeneca managers homed in was manufacturing.

Manufacturing was the Cinderella of the pharmaceuticals industry. All the glamour jobs, and much of the money, were elsewhere – in research and development, on which hundreds of millions of pounds were spent each year, and in marketing and sales, the consumer-facing activities. Between the back-room boffins and the front-line warriors, manufacturing – the process whereby the drugs were actually turned into pills and tablets – was regarded as a no-man's-land. Executives tried to avoid it altogether; where they could not avoid it, they spent as little time in it as possible before moving on to a more high-profile area. By the same token, companies traditionally invested enormous time and effort in the quest to improve productivity in R&D or the sales force. Manufacturing was seen as a commodity, low-value part of the process of transporting a drug from laboratory to GP's surgery.

Zeneca took a different view. Partly because of its origins in ICI, Britain's manufacturing flagship for much of the post-war era, and partly because of its quest to find fresh sources of competitive advantage, the company paid more attention to manufacturing than other drugs firms. It created the Zeneca Manufacturing Group, comprising the most senior manufacturing professionals across the company. At the end of 1994, almost eighteen months after the flotation, this group held a manufacturing conference in Ascot. Bill

Warnock, Zeneca's manufacturing strategy manager, was there. So was John Puttick, a former senior executive of PA Consulting and now one of Bhattacharyya's key lieutenants at Warwick. As a consultant, Puttick had already worked with a number of the Zeneca people at various different locations in the UK.

Warnock later described the background to the conference: 'We were looking at a whole series of changes and issues at that time,' he said. 'We were delayering the organisation fairly heavily, trying to become fleeter of foot and as competitive as possible in a fine chemicals industry that was changing quite rapidly. Part of that process was to look at the way we developed and educated people in manufacturing.'

Warnock and some of his colleagues recognised that Zeneca no longer had the luxury of indulging in old ICI practice, where senior people devoted considerable amounts of time to nurturing new graduate recruits, showing them the ropes in the drug-making process. 'We simply didn't have as many people around with as much time to spare,' Warnock said. 'So we looked around to see how we might fill that gap.'

The Zeneca people were aware of Bhattacharyya's Engineering Business Management concept. 'It appeared to be quite successful,' said Warnock. But no Zeneca manager had taken the course and the favourable impression was unsubstantiated by any detail. According to Clive Reynolds, Puttick's appearance at the Ascot conference made a big impact: 'John just set them alight,' Reynolds said. 'He became a stalwart partner in this.'

The Ascot conference crystallised Zeneca's thinking. 'We set up a task force of three people to think about what was required and to set down some sort of objectives for ourselves,' said Warnock. The recommendation was for a company-wide co-ordinated programme of education and training in manufacturing. 'It was decided that we should be retaining our best practices and sharing these, but that we should also look for some external inputs into this process as well,' Warnock said.

Zeneca also wanted to encourage its managers to take some individual responsibility for self-development: 'We wanted them to be doing things a little more proactively,' said Warnock. 'We encouraged them to seek out and take up opportunities and become more dynamic in their relationships with the business.' Scope for this kind of personal development was another element required from the academic partner that the company wanted.

A final group of three senior managers was formed to make the selection of Zeneca's external partner. The trio represented the three facets of Zeneca's business – pharmaceuticals, represented on this group by Mike Varo; agrochemicals, represented by Larry Lapple; and specialities – pharma-related speciality chemicals – which was Warnock's territory. Most of the institutions they considered were in Britain: 'Although we wanted in the longer term to stretch this globally, the UK was the most important area in manufacturing for us,' Warnock said. The Cranfield Institute of Management was one of the centres they looked at, but 'We decided fairly quickly on Warwick,' Warnock recalled.

At first sight, WMG might have seemed a slightly unlikely choice for a process-based company such as Zeneca. As Warnock said: 'At that time, and even to some extent still today, there was a lot available in universities to meet the needs of engineering and manufacturing people. There were, and are, plenty of aerospace, automotive, metal-bashing type of things. But there was not, at that time, anything for process industries. Even when you got techniques like MRP2 [Manufacturing Resource Planning], everything was geared to engineering. The principles are just as relevant for process industries, but these programmes didn't talk the right language; they were not appropriate to how the process industries ran.' Warwick was not immune from the general shortcomings. 'Good as it was, Engineering Business Management was not tailor-made for us. We could not just sink people in it – if we had been able to, we would have done so,' Warnock said.

Where WMG scored decisively was in its flexibility, its open-mindedness – its passion for partnership. As Warnock and his two colleagues headed towards Warwick on their fact-finding mission, they found Warwick moving towards them. Inspired by Bhattachar-yya's drive for expansion and urged forward by Clive Reynolds, the Group had developed a plan for horizontal diversification from the engineering and manufacturing sectors into the process industry. 'We had been trying to get PBM – Process Business Management – going,' said Reynolds. 'We targeted ICI, among others. That was the origin of John Puttick's appearance at the Ascot conference.'

But like many diversifying companies, before and since, WMG struggled to attract customers for its new venture. Tim Bridgeman, who later took over direction of the Zeneca programme from Reynolds, said: 'There appeared to be a lot of synergy with the teaching work we were doing, and also in terms of the research work that we were expanding at that time. And we did have considerable initial interest from ICI and others. But when push came to shove, it was difficult to get the programme launched. There were lots of questions.'

Bridgeman concluded that: 'The process industry does not have a history of investing in the development of its people. Yes, it spends a lot of time on process training – health and safety, operations, parameters. But interest in personal development does not seem to be in the culture of the industry, and that shows through.'

Warnock and his colleagues knew that they were breaking that mould. But just as WMG found it hard to establish a franchise in the process industry, so the Zeneca group quickly discovered that their ideas were more easily conceived than implemented. 'Having selected Warwick, we sat down with Clive Reynolds and his team to try to define and develop some sort of co-ordinated programme of education,' Warnock said. 'At first, we thought of it as a list of topics, but that didn't work and we had to go a little deeper. We started to think quite fundamentally about what we wanted. It was a fairly fraught and difficult process.'

That was not because there was any divergence of objectives

between Zeneca and WMG. Indeed, Warnock and his colleagues shared Reynolds' aspiration to attract a group of process companies to the course that was designed. 'We didn't actually want this to be Zeneca only,' said Warnock. 'We had felt much of our training in the past had been quite good, but one of its defects was that, because it was in-house, it was a little introspective. That was cutting our people off from one of the benefits of such education – the chance to find out what was going on more widely in the industry. We were happy to have a process business management course in which Zeneca would be just one of the participants.'

But it was now late 1995, and life for British manufacturers – and process industry companies – was getting harder. The artificial boost to competitiveness caused by the pound's collapse in the wake of so-called Black Wednesday – 18 September 1993, when sterling had been forced out of the Exchange Rate Mechanism of the European Union – had been deflated by the resurgence of the UK economy. Liberated from the shackles imposed by the ERM, and with the 1980s boom and bust a fading memory, the economy entered a new growth phase.

This time, unlike the 1980s, the benefits of the Thatcher revolution – flexible financial and labour markets and the freedom of management to manage – were not compromised by an inflationary spiral. A chastened consumer, sound fiscal and monetary policies, and the increasing spread of globalisation combined to create the most benign economic conditions for many decades. Soon, the pound began to rise as international investors realised that the British economy had incorporated many characteristics of its larger US counterpart.

By contrast, the Deutschmark, for decades the European currency of choice for investors seeking an alternative to the dollar, progressively lost its integrity and authority as Germany continued to struggle with the consequences of the ultimate merger – national reunification. Having plummeted to less than DM2.20 in the immediate aftermath of Black Wednesday – rechristened White

Wednesday by *The Sunday Times* – the pound began a sustained revival. By mid-decade it was back above DM2.50. In 1996, it reached DM2.60. And it did not stop there.

For manufacturers in Britain, sterling's revival had one benevolent effect: it helped to restrain the cost of bought-in raw materials, most of them priced in dollars. But for exporters to continental Europe, and for firms in the UK exposed to competition from continental European imports, the weakening of the Deutschmark – which dragged down the other European currencies – created growing pressures. Despite the reforms of the 1980s, one old habit died hard in UK plc: the habitual dependence on exchange rate depreciation to maintain competitiveness. Now, with each pfennig gain by the pound, that protection was being relentlessly stripped away. In the process, the basic shortcomings of British manufacturing industry – its relatively under-educated, under-skilled management and its technological weakness – were increasingly exposed.

Thought leaders such as Bhattacharyya, who had always argued that Britain must improve its essential competitiveness in product and process, saw this trend as fundamentally healthy. It would drive British companies to move up the value chain, to develop more technically advanced products and improve their commercialisation. But many companies found themselves struggling to cope with the new terms of trade. They – companies such as ICI, British Steel, Pilkington, Coats Viyella and Courtaulds – were subjected to intense pressures, pressure that flowed down their supply chains. The reaction of many firms was classically short-termist: they circled the wagons and started to cut back – on R&D, on capital investment and on the size of their workforces. And they turned their backs on the kind of secular, structural investments that they needed to survive in their current form. The WMG–Zeneca concept of Process Business Management, whatever the longer-term benefits it promised to confer, was seen as a luxury. Initial enthusiasm shown by several companies approached by WMG and Zeneca gradually evaporated.

'The manufacturing climate became rather chillier, and the rest all lost interest and felt that they couldn't resource it,' recalled Warnock. 'We still thought it was right and wanted to go ahead, on our own if necessary. So that's what we did.' Zeneca was fortunate because the pharmaceuticals industry remained highly profitable, so that there was never any question of the company being unable to afford the WMG initiative. However, not all of its operations enjoyed the same kind of margins as the drugs business – specialities were under some pressure and agrochemicals even more so. Zeneca's unique willingness to persevere with the management education effort owed more to the vision of its leaders than to the wealth of its resources.

By 1997, the partners had defined what the company wanted: a core group of seven modules which covered the basics of manufacturing as it related to Zeneca. These modules – strategic decision-making; compliance management; operations management; management of people and the change process; performance evaluation and control; production process innovation; and application of technology management – constituted the heart of the programme, and to a large extent still do. However, Warnock added: 'We planned to go on and develop these with narrower and deeper components for those who wanted to take it further.'

The seven modules were highly relevant to Zeneca's day-to-day and week-to-week challenges. Compliance management, for instance, incorporated health and safety, environmental and regulatory elements – a crucial spectrum for the company. 'In the pharmaceuticals industry, compliance is a key issue,' said Warnock. 'Just take the regulatory authorities such as the American Federal Drug Administration – if you do not observe the proper authorisation processes it is quite possible to come to grief.' That was precisely what happened to Fisons, one of Zeneca's competitors at the time. In its dash to diversify into the sexy pharmaceuticals sphere from its solid but mundane fertiliser business, the company neglected to ensure that its manufacturing processes met the exacting FDA standards. The regulator promptly refused to allow commercial production of a drug on which Fisons had bet the ranch. The company crumbled, being forced to abandon its grandiose ambitions and instead to break itself up. For Fisons' peers, its fate was a salutary reminder of the importance of full and total compliance.

Design of the Zeneca modules reflected the equal nature of the partnership with WMG. After Warnock, his two colleagues and Reynolds' team had worked through the ideas, Zeneca brought in some of its key managers who were particularly expert in the relevant areas being covered. They refined the modules' content further. For WMG, Puttick also contributed significantly, notably to the first module, strategic decision-making. Puttick said later: 'This was the field that I had worked in with quite a few of them in their various locations. They were great guys to work with; action people who wanted to do things. So I was looking forward to the first running of the module.'

Teaching of the first module on the first course began in November 1997, with twenty Zeneca managers attending. Puttick quickly had a shock: 'We got this very cynical, somewhat arrogant and smug response – they turned into this nit-picking lot who didn't like the course menu, didn't want to wear a collar and tie in the dining room, etc. etc. We eventually got to the root of it – these guys hadn't really been fully briefed on why they were coming to Warwick. They got here and found they were signed up for a seven- or eight-module programme leading to an academic qualification which they didn't particularly want.'

To discover what made someone tick, Puttick would focus above all on what enthused the particular individual. He asked the Zeneca class what each person was really interested in. 'One told me, "I like developing teams of people",' Puttick recalled the following year. He responded: 'That's fine, but what if you were developing a team in a bank?' The man replied: 'I would be just as happy doing that in a bank as in Zeneca.' This was anathema to Puttick, who responded: 'I certainly wouldn't, because all my life I wanted to be involved with making things.' But the response spoke volumes to Puttick: 'We had identified the culture in Zeneca that said, if you were in manufacturing, you were a bit of a failure – the aspiration was to get into the "proper" business.'

John Puttick died, after a long illness, in 1999. By that time, the bad start to the pioneering Zeneca programme was a distant memory. He, Reynolds, Bridgeman, Warnock and the others persevered with their partnership. They worked the tensions through and out of the system. Bridgeman said: 'With all dedicated programmes, we spend a lot of time working with the organisation concerned up front, determining what functionality and objectives we are trying to achieve with the target population. Invariably, they then send you atypical people for the first programme. Zeneca were no different.

'In some ways, that works quite well. It means that you put a lot of stress in the early modules on making sure that they are right and will meet what the company requires. But the early participants have to understand that they are there almost as part of the design process, literally as the pilots. They aren't getting the finished product; they are helping you to attain that.'

Once the teething troubles were ironed out, the focus shifted to the fundamental challenge. Bridgeman said: 'We had to establish the importance of the manufacturing function within a process industry. Within the industry, it's good that you generally don't get to the top unless you have actually been through manufacturing. But a lot of people appear to think, "I have done my two years stint in manufacturing – how fast can I go out and do something really important?"'

'There was an attitude – I'm not sure if it came from the days inside ICI – that "We are good, aren't we, because we make a lot of money." The answer to that was, "Yes, you are, but you are missing something." The Zeneca people came to realise that, although their manufacturing facilities weren't poor, and although manufacturing made quite good profits, there was an opportunity here to discover how to make a whole lot more.'

The partners recognised very quickly that the issue here was not academic qualification. 'The programme was aligned to the part-time certificate level,' said Bridgeman. 'A company such as Zeneca does not need a programme with an academic qualification, because its people are already well qualified. It's the rigour acquired through the academic process that they believe they will benefit from.'

In other words, WMG's diversification into the process plant sector with the Zeneca venture subjected Bhattacharyya's first principle – education for industry – to its most demanding challenge yet. 'You have to ensure that the assessments, the assignments, the projects are industrially relevant,' said Bridgeman. 'There is a tension between what's required in an academic environment and what is needed from a pure business report – I call it the integrative context.

'It's not enough, for example, to tell me that this is how you introduce Statistical Process Control in this process within the industry. What I need to understand is why SPC is the most appropriate form of quality control in this instance, and how it is best applied. What that demonstrates to me, what we are talking about here, is the difference between training – which WMG does not do – and education, which we most definitely do.'

Thus, while the Zeneca programme stretched the WMG people, it also provided the purest vindication for the Warwick way. It defined more clearly than any existing programme or partnership what made Bhattacharyya's ethic not only different, but better than the conventional academic approach to industry.

'We learned how best to apply the quality principle,' Bridgeman said. 'How to identify the most appropriate tool and technique in that particular industry. That comes from education. We quite often start off with a bit of tension between ourselves and the participants, simply because we won't accept a bullet-point industrial report. We tell the course participants that they have to show their logic and argument. But almost universally, by the end of the programme they accept the logic and the value of this.'

The Zeneca partnership also highlighted WMG's ability to add value to a manufacturing system that differed markedly from that of other industries. The UK pharmaceuticals sector came from the opposite end of the manufacturing spectrum to the mass-production car industry with which, through Rover, Bhattacharyya and his colleagues worked for two decades on techniques such as cellular manufacture. There was no large-scale manufacture on long-run production lines in huge factories; pharmaceuticals were made in low quantities by batch production at relatively small plants. This helped immunise the pharma companies from the labour unrest that dogged the engineering sector until the 1980s. However, once the Thatcher government's industrial relations reforms began to work through, eradicating wildcat strikes, secondary pickets and the rest, the continuity achieved in chemistry-based manufacturing had a reverse and less positive effect. Its insularity now became more of a weakness than a strength.

Awareness of this shortcoming was one motivation for Zeneca's original alliance with Warwick. As its exposure to WMG's engineering experience deepened, Zeneca began to rethink its industry's traditional manufacturing structures. One of the key benefits for Zeneca of the association with Warwick was the ability to access the organisation's profound knowledge base in manufacturing systems. 'The thing that worried me in chemical manufacturing was that it hadn't changed as much as it probably could have done,' said Warnock. 'Until very recently, the approach was quite traditional – you tailored processes to existing plant and equipment. The attitude was that here was the way we have done things, we know this works and we'll make it fit.

'That can't be right. We have changed to a much more fundamental approach. Now we ask ourselves what the chemistry requires, what the business requires – what would be good in those terms. And there is a whole lot more to go for. I believe we will see far smaller plant, maybe even on a micro scale, together with far more continuous production as opposed to batch processes. That adds up to far more flexibility. Instead of single-product batch runs as in the days of ICI, we are now into whole new businesses like genetics, making DNA modules where a year's production might be a couple of kilograms. You need a new philosophy of manufacturing to handle that.'

The need to master the challenge of manufacturing miniaturisation was compounded by the competition presented by the developing world. 'There are all sorts of pressures on manufacturing costs,' said Warnock. 'Countries such as South Korea, China and India have become very capable manufacturers, and they are creating huge pressures because of their capital and operating cost advantages. If we can't do things in a more clever way, then it will be progressively more difficult to compete with their wage rates.' There was a lot at stake in terms of job and wealth creation. In 2001, about half the company's fifty manufacturing locations were in western Europe, with many of the plants in Britain, where more than 10,000 people were employed. This was the constituency of the Zeneca–Warwick partnership.

In early 1999, the dimensions of the partnership were transformed by a corporate mega-deal. Contrary to all previous expectations, this was not a takeover of Zeneca by a predator. Instead, it was a merger of equals between the British group and the Swedish company Astra, best known for its Losec anti-ulcer drug (known as Prilosec in the US), the world's top-selling medicine. AstraZeneca was based in Britain and Zeneca's Tom McKillop was appointed chief executive. After the years of doubt about Zeneca's long-term independence, the deal was both a confirmation of its success in the post-ICI era and a gateway to a new phase of development.

There was no move to change a winning formula, a policy which certainly applied to the WMG relationship. 'Both Zeneca and Astra people took the view that the Warwick programme seemed just as relevant for them after the merger,' said Warnock. The most notable change was that the number of candidates for the courses multiplied overnight: 'Quite a few people from Sweden immediately registered an interest in participating when they saw what the programme looked like.'

Relevance was a vital ingredient of the course. It was provided by a joint Zeneca–WMG steering group which consistently monitored the content of the programmes and the feedback from them. Two modules in particular – production process innovation, and application of technology management – were adjusted as the programme developed. Warnock regarded technology management as one of the most successful units. 'Right from the beginning, we were determined that the modules should always be fully up to date and never become obsolescent,' he said. The steering group, comprising between three and five people, meets twice a year to review reaction to the modules and to refresh them if necessary.

Warwick executives recognised that the programme's success owed much to AstraZeneca's proactivity. 'AstraZeneca is a very good organisation with a commitment to making things happen,' said Bridgeman. 'A very important decision was their appointment of a programme manager to oversee all aspects of the course.' Warnock is the fourth such manager, following on from Mike Foot, who held the post for some time. The course participants are typically aged between twenty-five and thirty-five, with around six years in the company. They fall into two main categories: the younger ones are mostly graduate engineers – in chemical or other branches of engineering – while the more mature members are first line managers who have risen through the ranks or have joined the company without academic qualifications. WMG and AstraZeneca believe the course's ability to encompass both streams is a clear measure of its success.

Participants report rapid payback from their learning experience. Warnock said: 'They talk about making immediate cost savings, enhancing operations, finding newer ways of doing things, forming better relationships with other parts of the organisation, having improved vision of how the whole business operates. But even with all that, they probably see most of the benefits developing longer-term rather than on day one.'

Apart from improving each manager's understanding of manufacturing issues, the programme has also enhanced the status of manufacturing within the company. 'People have continued to see manufacturing as one of the less sexy parts of the company's activities, and IT and marketing as more attractive areas,' said Warnock. 'Even some of our engineers do manufacturing for two or three years and then want to be off to a business role. The WMG programme has helped to counter that. People are seeing more valuable, interesting and longer-term careers in manufacturing.'

The corollary also applies: a spell in manufacturing is now seen as almost mandatory for aspirants to top executive positions. 'The programme gets them something they can clearly see as career-broadening,' said Warnock. 'The contribution manufacturing is now making to business development is significantly greater than it was when we started. Of course, R&D is crucially important. However, people are now much more aware that we are at the high technology end of industry generally, and dependent on innovation in more than the product sense.'

The programme's definition has widened horizons in other respects. It has facilitated internationalisation in the company, through the increasing mix of people on the courses. This effect came about as much by accident as design. 'Once the WMG partnership was in place, we identified that the next most important manufacturing centre was the US,' Warnock recalled. AstraZeneca set about finding an academic partner there which could fulfil a role similar to that of Warwick for its European operations. The University of Delaware was selected, but before the programme there could get under way, one of AstraZeneca's key American manufacturing managers decided to put it on hold while he focused on other priorities. Warnock and his colleagues therefore decided to send the American managers who wanted to participate in a programme to Warwick.

When the US operation later changed its mind and decided that it wanted to promote a manufacturing education programme, the feedback from Warwick course participants was such that it was decided to continue sending to WMG. Almost unintentionally, the programme had gone transatlantic. By 2001, a couple of Warwick modules were being run in the US. In 2001, AstraZeneca was also examining an extension of the programme to Asia-Pacific, with Hong Kong or Singapore seen as favoured locations for module teaching.

The programme multiplied its membership in another way. In June 1999, shortly after the merger, the company decided to spin off the specialities business – whose products included leather coatings, colours, resins and biocides – into a leveraged buy-out (LBO) under the name Avecia. Six months later, AstraZeneca implemented a still-larger demerger, combining its agrochemicals operation with that of its Swiss rival Novartis to form a publicly quoted group called Syngenta. In late 2001, the combined value of the two public companies was almost £60 billion – £4 billion for Syngenta, while AstraZeneca was worth more than £55 billion.

Both the new groups, together with the now pure pharma AstraZeneca, continued to send candidates to the Warwick programme. This makes the WMG partnership unique, because it is the only activity in which all three constituents of the original group continue to participate. The steering group had to make some adjustments, said Warnock. 'The course uses live, up-to-date examples of manufacturing practice, so now that we are three companies and to an extent competitive with each other, we have had to make the examples a little more general to avoid any risk of proprietary information leaking out.' The committee also kept a close eye on course content to ensure that 'the programme didn't become skewed towards one party or another'.

They need not have worried. 'We thought it might be a real risk, but it doesn't seem to have materialised at all,' Warnock, who had moved into the Avecia specialities side, said in late 2001. 'Even though our main business drivers are different, the programme is still seen by each of us as fully relevant. It's quite remarkable really.' The WMG view was characteristically distinguished by professional understatement. Bridgeman said: 'The fact that all three businesses continued to participate showed the quality of the programme and the commitment of the companies.'

It did, but it was not quite the full story. WMG had achieved multi-company recognition for its process plant initiative, only not quite in the way that it had intended. Ironically, in 2000 the demonstrable success of the Zeneca venture attracted a request by Accordis, the fibres group, for a dual management development programme, one for fast-track and the other for senior managers – the first such programme that Warwick had been asked to run for fifteen years. Ironically, because Accordis was the product of the acquisition by the Dutch group Akzo Nobel of Courtaulds – the company whose demerger had encouraged the ICI split to create Zeneca.

Accordis's interest emphasised the value of the WMG–Zeneca relationship. Warwick's association with Zeneca in the crucial years as the British group grew up, out of the takeover shadows and into a multi-faceted global leader, provided a role model for academic–industrial partnership. By staying with WMG, each member of the AstraZeneca family was acknowledging that fact. They were paying Warwick what, within the terms and aims of that partnership, was a supreme compliment.

Chapter Seven

Into Africa – the South African Assignment

It is a sunny afternoon in Stanton, on the outskirts of Johannesburg. In the boardroom of Eskom, South Africa's electricity utility, a group of industrialists and educationists are seated round a huge circular table.

The object of their attention is Fernando Simoes, an Eskom fitter, who is delivering a presentation entitled 'Designing and Implementing a Knowledge Management Programme'. For Simoes, who has been identified by Eskom as having good management potential, the event is a nerve-racking but essential stage on his route to a Master of Science qualification in WMG's Engineering Business Management degree course.

Among those listening intently to Simoes's presentation is one of the key figures in what is, without doubt, the most ambitious project Bhattacharyya and his team have ever undertaken. Roy

Marcus, former Dean of Engineering at Witwatersrand, South Africa's foremost university, and now a private-sector education entrepreneur, is Bhattacharyya's South African partner.

It was Marcus who, after the release of Nelson Mandela in 1990, was appointed by the government of F.W. de Klerk to lead an inquiry into the state of the country's manufacturing sector, its needs and priorities. It was clear to everyone involved that a new world was coming: a world of social, political and economic liberalisation.

Just as the iron curtain of apartheid was being lifted, so South Africa's fortress economy, in which indigenous companies could shelter behind high tariff barriers and strict exchange controls, was also being liberalised. The ramifications for industrial competitiveness were enormous. A protected economy with a closed management class would be exposed to winds of international competition and domestic pressure for the development of a new managerial population, embracing the previously deprived and disadvantaged black and coloured majority.

It was clear to Marcus that South African industry's most obvious and pressing need was for management education: a programme that could transfer knowledge rapidly and on a wide scale to both the aspiring black and coloured and the newly exposed white management ranks.

'We surveyed the world,' said Marcus. 'We probably went to every leading British academic institution, plus the United States, Australia and Canada. One of the places we visited was Warwick. I met Kumar Bhattacharyya and realised that his was the model that would have to be introduced in South Africa.

'Unlike almost every other institution, including MIT, which we also visited, he had proved that he could transfer the Warwick Way to developing countries while also tailoring his programmes to the needs of the local user.'

Marcus went to see Bhattacharyya. 'I tried to persuade him to bring the Warwick model to South Africa. He said, "Never." He would not consider taking Warwick to South Africa until the government had changed.'

A disappointed Marcus returned home, where, as president of the national engineering association, he devised what he called The Top 100 programme, a project aimed at identifying the country's technology leaders. 'We were looking for a suitably well-known international personality to come here and launch the programme,' said Marcus.

'Kumar reluctantly agreed to come out here, because he felt the notion of Technology Top 100 was a good one – not because he wanted any identification with South Africa. That further convinced us that we had to get Warwick into South Africa, and I asked him to give me the chance to run WMG programmes in South Africa. Again, he said "No way."'

That was how matters stood until shortly after the historic general election of 1994, which swept Mandela to power. The election ushered in Ben Ngubane to head the Ministry of Science, Technology, Arts and Culture.

Ngubane brought considerable authority to the post. In February 1995, the new South African government concluded a joint scientific research agreement with the British government, called the Fifth Framework, which agreed joint funding for various programmes. Britain's science and technology minister flew to South Africa to sign the agreement.

Ngubane then became the first science minister from the southern hemisphere to be invited to give the Zuckerman Lecture to the Royal Society. The invitation reflected the close ties between the Society and the new South African government, which consulted the RS over the issue of science education in schools. Ngubane was told of the previous attempts to attract Bhattacharyya to South Africa. He decided to pay the WMG founder-director a visit.

'I made a return visit to look at the UK's science base,' Ngubane said. 'Through our High Commission in London, I asked to go to Warwick. This was my first encounter with Kumar Bhattacharyya.'

The only slot available in Ngubane's packed schedule was a Saturday afternoon. When he arrived at the WMG centre, he found that Bhattacharyya had arranged for the whole team to be present. 'It was tremendous,' Ngubane said.

Re-enter Roy Marcus, by now running his private venture Morgan Education Technologies, with his partner Richard Pike. The pair agreed that the Warwick management development programmes would be supremely relevant to South Africa. 'I wrote to Kumar, because I had got to know him quite well,' said Marcus. 'He invited me over, sat on the couch in his office at the engineering department, and said: "If you get the support of the South African government, then you can have the WMG programme."'

Because of Ngubane's enthusiasm for WMG, Marcus found himself pushing at an open door. Bhattacharyya's institution was seen, properly, as a paragon of excellence amid a sea of mediocre MBA offerings that was swamping South Africa.

In the wake of apartheid's fall and black empowerment, the country was regarded by foreign universities as one vast sales opportunity. Soon, South Africa was being flooded by cheap imports of overseas MBA courses, the vast majority – such as that advanced by Britain's Slough-based Thames Valley University – of highly dubious quality. So concerned did the government become that in late 2000, after two years in which the MBA market had inflated by 82 per cent, it was driven to announce a crackdown on the uncontrolled MBA invasion. The Department of Education introduced a registration system under which programmes offered by private higher education institutions had to be accredited by the national qualifications authority.

'What we are seeing is MBA dumping,' said one South African business school director. 'Some foreign institutions are just feeding off a brand name to milk the South African market. MBAs become just money-making schemes, taught by lecturers who are not good enough, taking on students who would not get accepted anywhere else, with very poor examination standards.'

The government's attack on MBA courses was controversial – reputable institutions in Britain and elsewhere were, at least initially, lumped in with the many indifferent MBA sources. But in the context of the government's reaction, Bhattacharyya's disdain for the MBA concept emphasised the differentiation between the indiscriminate MBA influx and WMG's own work in South Africa, which was embraced and sponsored at the highest ministerial levels.

Greg van Wyk, training and development manager for BMW South Africa and one of the relatively few private-sector participants in a WMG master's, said in mid-2000: 'South Africa has had a wealth of MBA courses since 1994, and there has been a lot of scamming.

'We have a backlog in education and people are prepared to grab anything that looks internationally acceptable. So if someone comes from Australia or the United States, they look international. To have a reputable institution like Warwick in the midst of that is helpful.'

From the outset, the WMG programme was the most expensive management education programme in the country – by 2000, the doctorate course cost around R85,000, at the time about £8,500. But by then, it could also claim to be the most popular such programme in South Africa.

The WMG course in engineering business management started in 1995 with twenty-two students. Almost all were from the public sector, although there was a smattering of private sector managers, with the single largest contingent coming from the state-owned power utility Eskom. Telkom South Africa, the state telecoms company, also sent several managers.

Allen Morgan, Eskom's chief executive, was an early convert to the WMG cause. Morgan, a veteran of the electricity supply industry, saw great opportunities for Eskom, both in the new South

Africa and beyond its boundaries. Eskom, he believed, could both dramatically raise the level of its performance at home and, over time, become an influential player on the world electricity scene.

The utility also faced a daunting task: affirmative action, the Mandela government policy for black advancement, posed a huge challenge of both quantitative and qualitative employee development. More than 96 per cent of Eskom's senior and middle managers were white. To meet the objectives of affirmative action, that percentage would have to be radically reduced. The inevitable turnover that would be involved could be massively destablising unless handled with extreme care.

At the same time, Eskom was charged with fulfilling another key government commitment: electrification of the African homelands, whose infrastructure had been largely ignored by the apartheid regime. The electrification project was a cornerstone of the hugely ambitious reconstruction and development programme to which the new government had committed itself, and which involved both the parastatals, the state-owned enterprises and the largest private-sector companies.

Eskom's self-set objective was daunting: 1.75m homes were to be electrified in five years. That equated to 350,000 homes a year. Given the massive infrastructure deficit in the areas where the work had to be done, this programme would place intense pressure on the Eskom management.

Morgan knew that the group's chances of meeting these exacting demands would be made or marred by its middle managers. Their ranks were already being thinned significantly – within five years, the number was down from more than 7,000 to 4,900 as part of a group-wide streamlining that cut the workforce from 67,000 to 40,000 staff. But job-cutting was just a first base; the toughest task lay in upgrading the quality of the managers that remained. 'Middle management is the most important layer in an organisation,' said Morgan. 'If those people aren't performing, you are dead.'

After being briefed by Marcus, Morgan concluded that Bhatta-charyya's programme offered something that Eskom could not obtain from conventional MBA courses. A reassuring coincidence was WMG's physical proximity at Coventry to the head offices of both National Grid, the privatised owner of Britain's electricity transmission network, and PowerGen, one of the two large generators privatised by the Thatcher government. Their headquarters stood cheek by jowl with the Warwick University campus and Bhattacharyya was well acquainted with the management challenges that both had faced in their establishment as private-sector companies.

'We had to ensure that, while we had local examples of good practice, we also brought in an international flavour, because we wanted an exchange of experiences,' Morgan said. 'Whether they were appropriate to your circumstances or not, we wanted to share. You can work almost anywhere in the electricity supply industry and the issues you are facing are almost identical. The whole world is going through a globalisation process. Visiting lecturers bring that perspective as well.'

The other main element of Bhattacharyya's approach that attracted Morgan was its intensely practical integration of technical and financial management education. 'Even the individual working in Treasury needs to understand the business he's operating in,' Morgan said. 'If one looks at the nature of the Warwick programme and the assignments the individuals have been given, it provides that broad context.'

From its early days, the WMG course also attracted individual high-flyers in South African industry. Caylene van Zyl, twenty-five at the time she enrolled, was a logistics manager with Nampak, the second-largest packaging group in the southern hemisphere. Van Zyl had an electronics degree and had cut her teeth in business as a management consultant with Ernst & Young, but after joining Nampak she realised that she really needed to study industrial engineering.

She looked at many of the MBA courses now on offer, but was generally unimpressed. 'A friend of mine asked whether I had heard of the Warwick programme, so I called Roy Marcus. It looked very expensive and I was unsure.' With characteristic thoroughness, van Zyl set about researching WMG. Her job was taking her overseas for a spell, so she went to the *Economist* in London, visited WMG and checked its references. Satisfied, she enrolled in November 1996, just over a year after the initial course.

'Coming from a consulting environment, I was challenged for the first three months,' she recalled. 'After that, I wasn't so challenged. But I read a lot, I went and found out extra stuff. It's really about promoting understanding – when you understand a concept, you add more concepts to it. A big plus for the programme is that you get away and learn, then come back to your job and implement – instead of going away, learning, then reading a textbook and writing an exam.'

Bhattacharyya's first principle – that what the student learns should have immediate commercial relevance to his or her company – translated seamlessly to South Africa. Van Zyl found that her dissertation – *Nampak Ltd: a new business model for the virtual economy* – was directly applicable to her business environment. The board director to whom she reported in her logistics role was also her course supervisor.

And just as Bhattacharyya's precepts found a ready home in Johannesburg, so his vision of manufacturing industry's future found resonance in the conclusions of the young, upwardly mobile manager. After working her way through modules including logistics, supply chain, marketing and strategy, van Zyl's thesis advocated that Nampak become more customer- and market-focused. It also identified that the growing fusion of business and information technology strategy would drive mass customisation, manufacturing out-sourcing and internal streamlining to the point where 'you are cutting out a whole set of middle management'.

Like the pioneers who had enlisted on Bhattacharyya's first

145

courses in Britain or Hong Kong, van Zyl also had to learn to live with the singularity, the unconventionality of Bhattacharyya's approach. 'The MBA is widely recognised, so it carries more of a status. If I say that I've got an MBA, everyone understands. But if I say that I have an Engineering Business Management degree, people ask: "What's that?" Once I mention the name Warwick, though, people know the school.'

Part of the recognition problem, van Zyl believed, was the simple fact that the Warwick degree was focused on the manufacturing sector. Even in South Africa, whose economy is far from the services-dominated industrial society of Britain, that was a disadvantage, she said. 'A plus with the MBA is that it is general, so you can go into corporate finance if you want to. With Warwick, you must enjoy manufacturing because that's where it's focused. You aren't going to do a Warwick degree and then go into corporate finance. Fortunately, I love manufacturing.'

As the government's growing interest in the WMG programme highlighted, however, her definition was severe. Reuel Khosa, a former Unilever and Royal Dutch/Shell manager who took over as Eskom chairman in 1997 after running his own management consultancy for sixteen years, inherited the utility's involvement with Marcus and WMG. He subsequently enrolled on the master's programme.

'Initially, I resisted doing an engineering master's,' Khosa recalled. 'I couldn't fully contemplate why someone who emerges from humanities could claim to be doing an engineering degree. But it's meant for people working within an engineering environment, not necessarily engineers but people doing something within an establishment such as Eskom, which is positioning itself for going transnational and global.'

Here, as in Britain and elsewhere overseas, the empiricism of the Bhattacharyya approach to management education distinguished WMG. 'One of the things that actually commended Warwick is their practical approach,' said Khosa. 'This engineering master's is predicated on linking what you study with what you do in your job.

'An MBA tends to be more academic than practical. Whereas here, there are modules on finance, innovation, human resources. You are encouraged to look at your own situation and give it practical as well as academic expression.'

Khosa's arrival at Eskom reinforced the company's existing commitment, championed by Morgan, to the Warwick programme. Khosa said: 'I made common cause with the then-minister of public enterprises to ensure that not only should we provide training to those in dire need of it, but that we should also ensure multi-skilling to those who might be undiminished in their particular skill.

'From the outset, we emphasised the learning organisation. We felt it was the only way to maintain what leadership position we feel we have. Reinforcing the link with Warwick was going to get us the assurance of continual learning, while making sure that things didn't fall between the cracks as they might if we were doing things on our own.'

The South African perception that Bhattacharyya's approach was responsive and relevant to local conditions, rather than prescriptively handed down *ex cathedra*, had played an important part in the government's desire to import the Warwick programme. From a very early stage, Bhattacharyya and his team validated the perception, adding a new milestone to their track record of working successfully in developing countries. In at least one respect, the South African experience was proving the supreme vindication of Bhattacharyya's attitude. WMG was adept at tailoring programme content to the needs and strategies of individual companies. But this was the first time its methodology was being applied to a whole nation.

As a result of the verification of WMG's bona fides through the work with Eskom and some private-sector managers, a more ambitious design began to be shaped by the South African government and Bhattacharyya.

In 1997, the WMG chairman met Thabo Mbeki, Mandela's nominated successor. Mbeki had two priorities: to access universities in South Africa's historically disadvantaged areas, and to enhance the calibre of the country's entire cadre of public sector managers. The government aimed to equip state-owned enterprises – parastatals, as they are known – to cope with eventual privatisation. As ministers well knew, successful privatisations would have a double benefit for the country: they would both breed international confidence in South Africa and, by attracting foreign investors, make that confidence self-reinforcing.

The government gave its programme the umbrella title Growth, Employment and Redistribution – Gear for short. Mbeki wanted Bhattacharyya to help get South African industry into gear.

Project 2000 was launched by Mbeki on 13 October 1997 in Johannesburg. 'This initiative derives from our firm belief that training and skills development is one of the key ingredients necessary to enable those denied opportunities by apartheid to contribute to their own liberation and indeed, to the transformation of South Africa,' Mbeki told the press conference which was attended by, among others, Bhattacharyya, Khosa, Marcus and Pike.

'The accent is on time and relevancy, and not on sending people on programmes just for the sake of satisfying communities that something is being done on the training front,' Mbeki continued, adding that Bhattacharyya's involvement gave the government confidence that the programme would attain its objectives.

'What we have uncovered as we examined the unique integrated Warwick Manager Development Programme is a model which has made a singular contribution to the development of companies and countries around the world,' he said. 'It has been used as one of the major drivers of the Malaysian, Hong Kong, Thailand, Indian and, more recently, Chinese economic miracles.'

The partners in this hugely exacting enterprise did not have to make bricks entirely without straw. Ngubane said: 'The democratic government was lucky to inherit a very strong scientific and technological structure, as well as a culture of research and development. But it was on a very narrow base.'

But the main R&D effort, of necessity because of the expansionist Soviet-backed Angolan regime, had gone into the defence industry. South Africa built its own helicopters, armoured personnel carriers and other materiel. On the civil side, because of the trade embargoes imposed by many countries, research was aimed at import substitution.

'While this generated a lot of exports and skills, it was cut off from the mainstream outside world,' said Ngubane. 'So some of the products we inherited still needed very high tariff barriers to protect their industries. We saw this in the clothing sector. The minute tariffs went down, these industries collapsed because they couldn't stand the low-cost competition, particularly from Asia.'

The new government's answer was to create clusters for industrial development, supported by a broad base of suppliers and skills, while realigning its science priorities: 'The priorities of the day have changed,' said Ngubane. 'We don't now see any kind of external threat, but we see poverty, AIDS, poor education as the most immediate challenges.'

While Ngubane hoped that WMG's expertise in technology development could also be deployed in South Africa, in partnership with the country's Council for Strategic Industrial Research, his most immediate concern was that Warwick should help raise the managerial standard. 'We need managers in this country. There is a real shortfall, and when the economy picks up this very quickly becomes a glaring flaw. That is one reason why Warwick is so important.'

The first target area involving WMG and Marcus was to assist in the revitalisation of the weaker regions, so that they would become more self-sufficient and reduce the amount of public money that was needed to support them. At the Mbeki meeting, Bhattacharyya undertook to create linkages between Warwick, Morgan and four historically disadvantaged universities – KwaZulu-Natal University of Zululand, University of Transkei, University of the North and University of Durban Westville.

'The whole notion is to find certain areas in which these universities could initially develop centres of expertise, and in so doing to help the local communities,' said Marcus. Khosa explained: 'We were saying, "Look, with Warwick's help, we can actually leapfrog some of the things that have hamstrung you in terms of your development and work with you to make sure we bring you smiling into the twenty-first century."'

Among WMG's considerable menu of tools for academia–industry collaboration, its partners in excellence programme was to be particularly relevant. 'The partners in excellence programme for small, medium and micro businesses enables the universities to use their newly acquired skills to create opportunities for smaller enterprises in these regions,' said Marcus.

As important as WMG's focus and expertise in engineering were the general disciplines that the Warwick programme could inculcate into students from these neglected catchment areas. Khosa said: 'The idea was to focus more on master's level than PhD students. Students who were given practical exposure and experience in the study of manufacturing industry would, in the process, be provided with the requisite framework in which to think a lot more systematically about some of the challenges they were facing. They would also gain exposure to what Warwick is doing with other emerging economies, as well as its work in the developed world.' WMG would be equipping the students with a broad frame of reference as well as specific engineering know-how.

The circumstances of the four universities differed. Durban Westville, for instance, was the only one of the quartet that offered engineering as an undergraduate degree programme. 'It has the best black engineering department south of the Sahara,' said Marcus.

'But it was seriously struggling. There was, in fact, no way it could survive if it continued as it was.'

He was called in by the government to see what could be done at Westville. 'We realised that no form of remedial work was going to sort it out. We had to look for a paradigm shift of engineering education, because as long as Durban Westville was in direct competition with the traditional white universities, it had no chance.'

For an answer, Marcus again looked to one of the key learning weapons in WMG's armoury: 'I recommended that we look at the undergraduate partnership degree, suitably modified to meet South African requirements.'

Mapule Ramashala, Westville's vice-chancellor, went to War-wick to meet Bhattacharyya, who committed to help the university develop a modified partnership degree course and to support it with lecture visits from Warwick. The version that emerged, the International Partnership degree in engineering, was run by the university, but entirely on site inside the local companies where the students worked. 'The university can now compete on an international basis,' said Marcus. 'It is not hidebound by its geographical location.'

Several of the distinctive WMG features – flexibility, under-standing the needs of the customer and the ability and readiness to tailor programmes to those needs – were in evidence. The two biggest companies involved in the Durban programme were coal-mining and gold-mining companies. They wanted their managers to understand the intricacies as well as the principles of running a mine. WMG's modular approach enabled Marcus and Westville to develop three modules for each business, in conjunction with the industries concerned. They were then adopted as official industry programmes.

The focus in KwaZulu-Natal was different, and exemplified how the general disciplines intrinsic to the WMG programme could be as valuable as the detailed engineering curriculum. Here, Bhatta-charyya's first customers were the ministers who made up the provincial government.

The programme was launched by an invitation from Ben Ngubane to Bhattacharyya to present his programme to the KwaZulu cabinet. Marcus said: 'The objective of the programme here was to create a mindset with senior KwaZulu-Natal managers that they were operating government as a private sector operation. The programme was specifically designed around this aim, to change the mindset that said, "We are running something in the public sector".'

The target market might have been different from usual, but Bhattacharyya's celebrated modules could still be put to highly relevant use. 'The issues were: how to really understand the organisation's finances; how to deliver customer service and satisfaction, and so on,' Marcus said. 'The WMG modules were perfectly suited to this task.'

A similar approach was adopted in the Northern Province, where Nthoana M. Tau-Mzamane was the director of science and technology. She had some experience of British higher education – she had taken a PhD in agronomy at the University of Aberystwyth. The WMG programme, she recognised immediately, was a very different animal from the conventional degree course. 'There was an awareness of the programme because, by the time it came to us, it had already started in other provinces,' she recalled. 'Once we were run through what the programme was about, and what it wanted to achieve, it sounded very exciting to us for a number of reasons.'

The Northern Province cabinet liked the look of Engineering Business Management because of both its range – covering diploma, master's degree and doctorate – and its interaction of learning and practical application. 'It offered us an opportunity as a province to get ourselves through the higher education phase, but not in the usual way,' Tau-Mzamane said.

The usual way was for a student working in the provincial government to obtain a bursary, attend a university course, and return to their job. It was very much an individual enterprise, isolated from the rest of the person's department, let alone the wider administration. Moreover, while the student would be expected to benefit from a higher education experience, there was no guarantee that their learning would be of any practical application to the work on which they were now re-engaged.

By contrast, Tau-Mzamane thought, 'The Warwick programme appealed to me because I saw an opportunity to take a group of people working in my department, put them on the programme, and enable them to learn many things with people who had experience elsewhere of matters relevant to their jobs. When they interacted with the lecturer, they could learn about general principles but also create the opportunity for a more practical discussion. So they enjoyed individual enhancement, but they could also come back into the department in a sort of critical mass. Then they would be equipped to handle some of the challenges facing the department.'

Northern Province certainly faced some challenges. It had been thrown together by the new government from four former administrations, each with its own particular culture. 'People had to start to learn at once how to live with each other,' said Tau-Mzamane. 'That's very difficult.'

South Africa generally might have been relatively underdeveloped in management education, but Northern Province was underdeveloped by South African standards. Tau-Mzamane said: 'We had historic baggage – we were faced with the challenge of trying to catch up with the rest of South Africa at a time when the resources that we could focus on this task were no longer available, because so many people were wanting a piece of the national cake.'

The province's department chiefs, in charge of its strategic direction, had to 'define the strategic path in a way that could maximise our limited resources but also bring about visible changes in the life of the people in the province'.

In the context of this dual imperative, the Warwick programme's high yield – its tight structure, lack of flabbiness and focus on results – was extremely appropriate.

The rapid take-off achieved by the programme was helped by the fact that significant ground had already been laid to build a team ethic in the provincial government. During 1997, the province's premier had created a series of 'executive clusters' – infrastructural, social and economic – designed to promote inter-departmental concentration on key areas of activity, such as housing, education and finance.

'Once we were put into clusters, we had the beginnings of a common vision,' said Tau-Mzamane. 'We began to understand each other; we began to realise that we were all in this together.' The nascent team spirit allowed rapid diffusion and acceptance of the Warwick teaching. 'The head of public works soon got interested in the programme; so did the head of local government, the head of finance and economic affairs, and so on,' said Tau-Mzamane.

The programme contained change management and financial management courses, which were particularly relevant to the needs of the province. 'Historically, Northern Province had a number of government farms – estates which had been doing quite well to begin with but then started making losses,' Tau-Mzamane said.

'In the new dispensation, the government was not going to run any businesses like these. You had to be very creative in how you turned these around – it was part of your responsibilities to the people who had been accustomed to having these farms as a source of income. How do you package these things in the private sector? That was one question the Warwick programme addressed.' The course, she said, demystified the financial dimension: 'These things that were mysteries before I now found to be quite understandable.'

154

WMG's work in Asia's developing economies proved highly relevant. 'People came in and said, "Such and such a business in Malaysia or China did this – we are not suggesting that you do the same thing, but be innovative and you can solve apparently intractable problems."'

Tau-Mzamane soon found that she had the opportunity to apply those lessons on a national scale, and in the context of research and development. She was invited to become deputy director-general of Science and Technology, part of Ngubane's department. 'What I had learned helped a great deal when I came to the Centre of Industrial and Scientific Research and was in sessions with people from other departments and provinces,' she said.

She left the Northern Province programme in good shape. On 7 January 1998, Tony Blair announced, during a visit to Johannesburg that cemented his close relations with Nelson Mandela's government, a new phase in the Warwick–South Africa partnership.

Two International Competitiveness Centres were to be established, one in Northern Province, the other in KwaZulu-Natal to promote best management practice in the private-sector economy of the two provinces. Bhattacharyya, who was also present, commented: 'The new partnership agreements with business and government in South Africa will help enhance management skills in the battle for global competitiveness.'

At the same time, Bhattacharyya announced a new partnership agreement with Eskom. Khosa was by now convinced that Warwick had a lasting contribution to make to the company's development.

'The idea was to focus more on master's-level students than just PhDs. Our people would have practical exposure and experience in manufacturing industry-type study. They would be provided with the requisite framework in which to think a lot more systematically about some of the challenges that they were facing. They would gain exposure to what Warwick is doing with other emerging economies, as well as what it is doing with developed economies.'

By early 2000, there were more than a hundred Eskom people on the WMG course. Allen Morgan said: 'We haven't had any negative feedback from Eskom students; it's early days yet, but what we are getting from managers who have come out of the Warwick programme is a far better focus on technology management.'

Through Marcus and Pike, WMG has also made some very specific contributions to translating government policy on empowerment into reality. Among the most notable is what Khosa calls 'a very unique scheme that Warwick tailor-made for us'.

The two-year master's degree course, launched in October 1999, is aimed entirely at encouraging, identifying and promoting women into management positions. It is known as the '40 Women' programme, because that was the number selected from the 200 who applied, from throughout South Africa, when the scheme was launched. 'This is the first such scheme ever,' said Khosa. 'When we launched it, we invited all state-owned enterprises and a number of major corporations to publicise it.'

All candidates had to have a BSc. Some of the chosen forty worked for Eskom; many were unemployed; others, according to Science and Technology Minister Ngubane, would have become teachers – a laudable enough career, but one where women had an established role, in marked contrast to their position in industry. 'In Eskom, we had practically no women in management posts,' said Khosa. 'The industry has been very, very macho.'

Only one out of twelve Eskom executive directors was a woman, and about 15 per cent of the executive level just below director were female. Khosa said: 'We believe there is no reason why, when they are in a majority of the population, we should not reach 30 per cent female representation by 2005.' Eskom has committed to taking on all forty candidates, or however many succeed in obtaining their degree.

The programme content melds the WMG approach to engineering business management with life skills and other more general subjects. But the technocratic element remains the core. 'These women are not going to be engineers,' said Morgan. 'They will be technology managers. They will provide us with what we needed – role models in management positions in the organisation – very quickly.'

The 40 Women course was exceptional, even by the standards that WMG programme lecturers had encountered in South Africa. 'Their thirst for learning, their hunger for knowledge is extraordinary,' Pike said after six months of the course. 'To teach them is a truly humbling experience, because their reaction brings home the full meaning of self-improvement through education.'

But the course also exemplified, through the exceptional intensity of the learning experience it created, the wider impact of the Bhattacharyya influence on those who took the Warwick programme.

At Eskom, Khosa said: 'It's quite amazing. Most of the recruitment is not done any more by Morgan Institute or Warwick; it is done by the current candidates.'

Morgan added: 'We have one of our very prominent shop stewards on the Warwick master's at the moment. I've noticed quite a transformation in his understanding of technology, technology management and the business in general. You see diversity at work at its best in the Warwick classes.'

Marcus could cite specific examples of how the programme had created economic benefits: 'One woman from Standard Bank has saved the company R33m as a result of the project she did for her master's; an Eskom guy has saved the firm R30m.'

But he agreed with Morgan that the programme had a wider, deeper cultural influence than the technical mastery that it conferred on its participants. The key elements of Bhattacharyya's approach – its egalitarian, multi-cultural, interactive, practical and flexible principles – found supreme resonance in the challenges and aspirations of 'his' South African students.

'We have high-quality institutions in this country. But we are coming from a history where there was privilege, in terms of exposure to the scientific world as in many other areas, and where the other, larger category of people were merely told what they had to do,' observed Tau-Mzamane as she sat at a long table in her recently inherited Pretoria government office.

'There is a whole knowledge base that has come out of these institutions. It is part of the responsibility of this department to ensure that it can be accessed, now and progressively, by the others who were excluded from it. We are starting this process, but so far the flow of information is more of a transfer than a sharing. We want to link scientists to the real world – not to one world, but to the diverse world that South Africa is today. We hope the Warwick programme can be adapted to help advance that process.'

Marcus said: 'The critical thing about the Warwick programme in South Africa is its racial and gender mix. Where do you find one room where you have a cabinet minister sitting next to a chief executive in a non-hostile environment and you are talking about serious issues related to the development of South African government and the companies? That's what happens in the lecture rooms in Pretoria, Pietermaritzburg, Durban and Cape Town.'

Those lecture rooms were no ivory towers: they were prisms reflecting all aspects of the new South Africa. 'Sometimes on the doctorate programme there are more bodyguards than candidates,' said Marcus. That fact testified both to the high-level positions occupied by many participants – and to the pressing need for individual security.

By mid-2001, six years after the start of the first Warwick course, economic improvement was still a work in progress. The economy was forecast to grow at 3 per cent that year – ahead of most Western economies, but only half the pace that Mbeki had deemed necessary to correct the imbalances of the past.

In late June, Mbeki and several of his senior ministers visited Britain. While the President was being received by the Queen at Windsor Castle, weathering the dust clouds sent up by the parade of Household Cavalry, some of his ministers and their officials met with Bhattacharyya to review progress and assess priorities.

Mbeki was concerned that, despite government initiatives such as hefty investment in training programmes, sections of the private sector were not pulling their full weight. 'The economy continues to be dominated by these large corporations, which quite naturally because of their size and international activities have had to expand outwards,' he told the *Financial Times*. 'I understand that, but . . . half of the investors' minds follows the money.'

A different kind of gulf was noted by BMW's van Wyk. 'The public and private sectors have been miles apart,' he said. 'But now, under Mbeki, the public sector is becoming more business-minded in approach.' The private sector also had enormous scope for improved productivity and efficiency, he believed. 'There has been a lot of protection of South African business. That's falling away.'

WMG's role in enhancing the public sector's performance remained critical. 'The government can't continue to bear the cost [of unprofitable parastatal operations],' Katharine Butt of Business Map, an economic research company, remarked in early 2000. 'It's putting a strain on the country, and it's not encouraging to foreign investors to see how these parastatals are being run as an example of how South Africa is being run.'

Ben Smit, director of the Bureau for Economic Research at the University of Stellenbosch, said privatisation 'is a cornerstone of the policy path they have embarked on. If you want to see sustained growth, beyond the 3/3.5 per cent ceiling, privatisation is going to be important.' Telkom South Africa was slated for privatisation in 2002. Eskom was due to follow eventually.

Back in the dusty streets of Durban and the long corridors of power in Pretoria, the abiding impression was of a political, financial and industrial leadership racing against time and many hazards, from the AIDS epidemic to the regional headache caused by Robert Mugabe's state-sponsored terrorism in Zimbabwe.

Despite the heat, people seemed in a state of extreme urgency. It was as if they realised that failure rapidly to disseminate the seeds of inclusive prosperity would doom the country to be dragged back and down by its inner demons.

There could be no doubt that Bhattacharyya's group had become an integral part of that brave but formidable enterprise. Alan Curtis, Bhattacharyya's point man at Warwick for the South African venture, said the criteria that would determine WMG's success or otherwise were: 'How they perform in improving management for industry; in making the transfer to a free market economy; how well that's handled and how the companies themselves survive.'

But the programme could already record one achievement: in their extraordinarily close and sustained co-operation, WMG and the Mbeki administration had set a new benchmark for university –government partnership to advance the wealth of a nation.

Chapter Eight
Marconi Calling

The telephone rang on the desk of Sir Ernest Harrison, chairman of Racal Electronics. On the other end of the line was one of his top executives. 'I thought you would like to hear the statement that GEC has just issued,' the man said. 'It says the company is examining alternatives for the future of its Marconi electronic systems division.'

Few events had taken Harrison by surprise during an illustrious business career spanning almost half a century. But this time he was stunned. There was a sharp intake of breath and a brief pause. Then he said simply: 'Run that by me again.'

Between the lines of the statement, Harrison read that GEC was prepared to sell Marconi. His astonishment at the news that his arch-rival, the company with which he had competed for decades, was being put up for sale was echoed throughout British industry. Former GEC managers, who populated significant portions of UK plc's upper echelons, were flabbergasted that their old company had chosen to sell what everyone saw as the jewel in its crown.

For Rob Meakin, GEC's human resources director, the decision was even more momentous. Meakin was already grappling with the task of re-educating managers and engineers steeped in the hard school of old GEC, an ingrained culture which was overwhelmingly concerned with controlling costs rather than expanding sales and made few concessions to twenty-first century notions of human resource development. Under its legendary managing director Lord Weinstock, GEC's central staff divided their sprawling empire in order to rule it. Numbers, rather than people, came first. The message was: perform or leave. In the Weinstockian world, it was survival of the fittest. Personal development was not on the agenda.

Meakin's view was rather different: 'GEC's future success depends on the continued involvement and commitment of its people,' he said. The group would 'foster the creation of a world-class learning environment which – through openness and sharing information – encourages innovation and creativity and empowers people at all levels to take a greater part in business decision-making'. To denizens of old GEC, he might have been talking a foreign language.

'We've got to be a continuous learning organisation, so nobody can afford to sit back and say, "I've got my master's",' Meakin believed. 'You need something to continually grow and stretch people.' To develop that something, he turned to Kumar Bhattacharyya's Warwick Manufacturing Group with a programme that broke new ground in industry–university collaboration. In partnership with Warwick, New GEC was about to deliver a huge shock to the company's old system.

There could have been no greater manifestation of that shock, either externally or internally, than the sale of the group's largest single business. Marconi Electronic Systems had operating profits of more than £430m on sales of more than £3.5 billion – making it by far the largest business in the group, accounting for almost half

GEC's total sales and profits. From radar to avionics, from missiles to satellite technology, the operation was the heart of Weinstock's company.

But Weinstock had retired, and the new management team was led by George Simpson, whose previous posts included deputy chief executive of British Aerospace, chairman of Rover and chief executive of Lucas Industries.

Simpson knew that GEC, which had barely increased its sales in the past decade and had massively underperformed the stock market during that period, had to change. Investors wanted expansion – not in dividend income, which Weinstock had provided, but in capital growth, which he had not. Simpson understood the fundamental terms of his contract with the shareholders. The question was, how could he achieve their desired objective?

That was where Meakin and GEC's new finance director John Mayo, the two other key members of Simpson's new team, came in. Simpson had recruited Mayo, a former S.G. Warburg corporate financier, from the pharmaceuticals company Zeneca where he had held the finance portfolio since the company had been demerged from Imperial Chemical Industries. In physical distance, Mayo had not come far: Zeneca occupied the office just across the road from GEC in Stanhope Gate, Mayfair. But in his approach to the job, Mayo was light years from the conservative, what-we-have-we-keep ethos of Weinstock's old GEC.

Simpson did not know Mayo, but Meakin was an old friend and colleague. The pair had met in the early 1980s, when Simpson was running Coventry Climax, the forklift-trucks arm of British Leyland. As Simpson rapidly climbed the BL ladder, so did Meakin. Under Sir Graham Day, Simpson became the renamed Rover Group's chief executive and Meakin its personnel director.

Meakin soon met Bhattacharyya through the latter's long-standing work with Rover. At any one time, almost a hundred Rover engineers were working at WMG's Advanced Technology

Centre. 'That gave us a physical activity where we had Rover people on projects,' Meakin said. 'For new technology projects, that was a first in my experience: university and company working hand-in-glove.'

Bhattacharyya and his team were already intimately involved with Rover's effort to raise the skill levels of its engineering managers. Using the modular techniques that Bhattacharyya had pioneered, and a business excellence model devised by WMG, Meakin and Bhattacharyya now worked closely to improve the Rover managers and the management process.

Meakin recalled: 'At Rover, Kumar was doing a hell of a lot of work with Andy Barr [Rover's manufacturing director] on getting a foundation of a good and loyal group of young managers in place with leadership skills. He had defined a model for cell managers which included a different range of skills and aptitudes from that which had previously been seen as important.

'The model was not just about who was the best at such-and-such, but about developing genuine leadership skills. Sure, you have to have technological abilities and aptitudes, but you don't have to come from exactly that technical background.'

Bhattacharyya, said Meakin, 'enabled a whole generation of leaders to be identified because they were assessed and trained against that module. That gave us a lot of horsepower to use these new leaders to reshape the business. On one side, we took out 4,000 managers and yet we did not lack for leadership.'

In 1992, the development process culminated in the launch of a full engineering doctorate that was widely taken up in Rover. By the time of the BMW takeover of Rover two years later, Bhattacharyya and Meakin, who was then personnel director of BAE, were well advanced with a still more ambitious initiative to extend the engineering management education process to under-graduate level, but through a radical concept that went far beyond the conventional sandwich course.

They created what they called a partnership degree: a three-year engineering degree in which students would sit the same exams whether they were in employment or full-time in the Warwick engineering department. They would only attend Warwick for two or three days a week; the rest of the time, they would do their applied study wherever they worked at Rover. Students would have the option of an extra year to take their degree to master's level.

Winning approval for the partnership degree was far from easy. Bhattacharyya had to push hard to get the idea approved by the Warwick University senate, some of whose members were dubious about a degree-standard course that involved more work in the student's company than at the university. But once again, Bhattacharyya's powers of reasoning and persuasion won the senate around.

He was less successful with the engineering establishment, with whom he once more found himself at cross-purposes. The Institution of Mechanical Engineers refused to accredit the partnership programme because it was not entirely taught at a university. The course was expensive, because it needed a high ratio of Warwick staff to ensure that the work done inside Rover was of the required standard. This in turn made it difficult for WMG to persuade other companies to join the programme. But it was widely seen as a high-quality course, and attracted twenty students a year from Rover.

Meakin's in-depth experience of working with WMG came into play almost immediately after he joined Simpson at GEC in 1998. Simpson only just got his man: Meakin was on the point of joining Centrica, the supply business created from the demerger of British Gas and headed by Roy Gardner, ironically Marconi's former managing director.

Gardner knew Centrica faced a huge human resources challenge to create a new identity and dynamic culture out of what, in its latter stages, had been a badly battered company. He wanted Meakin, with his track record in change management, to lead the personal development strategy that would make such a transformation possible.

Much to Gardner's regret, Meakin opted to join Simpson. Once at Stanhope Gate, he wasted no time in reopening contact with Bhattacharyya. At this stage, the idea that GEC might sell Marconi was far from the minds of the new GEC team. But what Simpson, Meakin and co. did know was that the company mindset would have to be drastically changed.

In August 1998, the balance of the business shifted when GEC bought out Siemens, co-owner of the GPT telecommunications equipment joint venture, for £610m. GPT's biggest business was in public switching – traditional telephone exchanges, for which demand was decreasing as fixed-line voice traffic growth was superseded by the explosion in demand for data communications, the so-called data wave.

Then, in a neat move that Weinstock himself had wanted to make, Simpson combined the now wholly owned company with GEC's Italian arm, Marconi SpA. The Italian business had cutting-edge technology which, when combined with GPT, created the world leader in the field of Synchronous Digital Hierarchy (SDH) optical transmission equipment, at the time one of the fastest-growing segments in voice-based telecoms networks.

Many observers had reckoned that, rather than buying out Siemens, GEC would sell its share in GPT to the German leviathan. The reverse deal, conceived and executed by Simpson and Mayo, significantly altered the balance of the group and lent weight and urgency to Meakin's culture-change plans.

Then came the Marconi electronic systems announcement. It was timed by Simpson and Mayo to head off the threat of a mega-merger between BAE and Germany's DaimlerChrysler Aerospace (Dasa). Such a deal would kill the chances of a merger between GEC itself and BAE, something Simpson had discussed with BAE at least twice. It could also isolate Marconi. Simpson had explored in depth the possibility of a transatlantic union between GEC and

Lockheed Martin, America's largest defence contractor, but those talks were foundering. To realise full shareholder value for Marconi, he could sell the company to BAE – but to do that he had to move fast. The BAE-Dasa deal was almost done.

Just as this endgame was developing, Meakin and Bhattacharyya took a crucial step in the GEC metamorphosis. They announced the creation of a New Knowledge Partnership, providing for long-term co-operation between the company and WMG to develop the skills of GEC's people. The model was the Rover relationship, but this was to go much further afield, both geographically and in its content. In effect, GEC and Warwick planned to establish a company-wide virtual university.

The agreement attracted attention and commendation at the highest level. Tony Blair's Cabinet Office was an ardent advocate of closer relations between academia and industry, recognising that this was a linchpin of greater competitiveness in the emerging 'new economy'. Blair and his team knew both Simpson, who had been appointed a Labour peer, and Bhattacharyya, who had hosted a visit by Blair on the eve of the 1997 General Election. They saw the GEC–Warwick partnership as raising a standard for both industry and higher education to follow.

'Britain needs to be at the forefront of the new knowledge-driven economy,' Blair said. 'Many British companies are already rising to this challenge. More need to. That's why I welcome the New Knowledge Partnership between one of our main industrial companies, GEC, and one of our foremost academic industrial centres, the Warwick Manufacturing Group at the University of Warwick.

'Business must embrace this kind of cross-cutting partnership with academic and other organisations if we are to develop the skills we need as a country in a fiercely competitive world. We must move beyond old-style corporatism and free-market laissez-faire into new partnerships – between business and universities, and between business and government,' Blair said. 'Supporting the delivery of long-term macro-economic stability and improved educational standards, building the knowledge-driven economy is central to Britain's competitive future.'

Meakin had market-tested several universities, in both Europe and the United States, before coming back to Warwick. The search had highlighted Warwick's pre-eminence in Britain and the marked difference between its industry-friendly approach and the much more inflexible American attitude.

'For the well-funded top American universities, it hasn't been so essential to have close links with industry,' Meakin said. 'In the UK, people such as Kumar Bhattacharyya caught on very early to the fact that, if you really wanted to build a successful institution, you wanted funding that didn't come from government routes.

'By contrast, all the big Americans have lots of money. For undergraduate programmes, for instance, they will all say: "We've got just what you need" and pull out a sandwich course. You say, "This is not what I wanted; I want education inside the company." And they say, "Well, this is how we do it." With Kumar, when you say, "This isn't what I want," he says: "OK, tell me what you want and we'll find a way of delivering it."'

And that is what Bhattacharyya said when Meakin briefed him on his ideas for Marconi. 'We needed someone who would move forward fairly quickly and who we knew could deliver results,' Meakin said. 'Of course, you can go through the learning curve of working up a relationship with someone else. But Kumar Bhattacharyya has a proven record which says he is successful. My experience with him, working both in the UK and overseas, has been that he will deliver for you.

'He is one of those guys who, whenever and wherever you meet him, leaves you with an uncomfortable feeling and an itch that needs to be scratched. I always think, "I didn't really enjoy that conversation, and it was very challenging, but we could do something around that." He stimulates thought and challenges you. Why do it that way? Why not try it a different way? It is essential to keep changing, because the business we are in keeps changing. Kumar is right up with things.'

And within a few weeks, GEC really did change. On 19 January 1999, it agreed to sell Marconi electronic systems to BAE in a deal that valued the business at almost £8 billion. Even after the December statement, the reaction in Britain's electronics industry was one of bewilderment: 'I can't see the way ahead for GEC,' said one former Marconi manager who now ran another company. 'It has sold its only world-class business. To me, this looks like the end.'

It was, in fact, the end of the beginning. It dramatised what Simpson and co. had originally intended to be a quiet, albeit all-encompassing revolution. At the same time, it was a massive catalyst for further change.

Shorn of its prime business, GEC – which set about changing its name to Marconi, having retained the name after the BAE sale – was left with the GPT – Marconi SpA business, now renamed Communications and accounting for half group sales. GEC also had non-core businesses such as domestic appliances, and smaller core activities – Picker medical imagers, Gilbarco petrol pumps and Videojet ink printers – which were gathered into a division called Systems.

The sale to BAE crystallised the objectives of the soon-to-be-rechristened Marconi. The name suited the new group well, because it was now quite obvious that it had to re-create itself as a multinational group focused on the communications industry, using its significant financial resources to fund acquisitions in this field. For Simpson and Mayo at the deal-making end, and for Meakin at the human resource level, the sale of defence electronics both raised the stakes for the transformed company and concentrated the minds of its top management.

Some senior telecoms industrialists were dubious. One executive of Nortel Networks, the Canadian giant that had transformed itself, at great speed and expense, from an old-style public switching company into a voice, data and internet networks provider, said: 'They will either have to specialise or find a strong partner' – in other words, look to be bought out. Asked whether he thought the GEC metamorphosis was credible, a senior British Telecommunications manager said bluntly: 'No.'

Simpson and his team had certain factors in their favour. Thanks to the internet and the mobile phone boom, the telecoms equipment market was starting to take off. Marconi had a solid customer base in Europe, with BT the cornerstone of that base. And it had money: with about £10 billion to call on in cash and borrowing capacity, the company had the resources to buy a grub stake in the networking world. Provided Marconi could attain critical mass, both by expanding its narrow product range and by seizing a bridgehead in the world-leading US market, and then hold that ground, it would have an even chance of making the transition from old GEC.

The US foothold was quickly established: within three months of the BAE deal, Marconi bought an American network equipment company called Reltec for $2.1 billion. A month later came a much larger and more important deal: the purchase of the Pittsburgh-based Fore Systems for $4.5 billion.

Fore was expensive, but it brought Marconi a crucial stepping-stone into the new world of communications infrastructure. The company, founded by four graduates of Carnegie Mellon University in Pittsburgh, both broadened and modernised Marconi's product range. Among Fore's armoury of new-generation transmission technology were Asynchronous Transfer Mode (ATM) and Internet Protocol (IP) switching systems.

ATM was a key component in the kind of networks for which the corporate world was now clamouring: high-capacity, high-speed systems capable of transmitting both voice and data traffic. And IP network switches were essential for web-based voice, data and video communications. Simpson said that Fore 'adds the vital broadband switching element to our technology portfolio and allows us to participate fully in the fast-growing data networking market'.

But the significance of the deal went beyond the product level. For Meakin and WMG, the acquisition was equally important. It provided the necessary infrastructure to make their New Knowledge Partnership both truly international and at the forefront of management education in the e-business age. And it made the success of that partnership absolutely integral to the fortunes of the Marconi group.

By hugely deepening Marconi's immersion in the networking business, the Fore acquisition added a human resources dimension to the new group that had not been present before. The network components business was as different from traditional public switching as the term manufacturing, with its connotations of heavy plant and engineering, was from the digital world of technology.

Network developers such as Fore had much more in common with the computer software companies that inhabited Silicon Valley than with traditional telecommunications equipment producers, let alone the type of heavy industries such as steel that had once dominated the Pittsburgh landscape. Above all, therefore, the Fore deal transported Marconi across the threshold dividing the old industrial world from the new, knowledge-based industry of the future.

That knowledge was held personally – Marconi was now, in a way that GEC had never been, a people business. Most of GEC's assets had been tied up in heavy plant and equipment. Marconi's assets, by contrast, had brains, arms and legs – and could use them to walk out of the business.

Of the purchase price, only $500,000 had been in fixed assets. The other $4 billion was goodwill – the goodwill, you might say, of the highly skilled people who had created and developed Fore. Simpson's greatest fear was that, after the acquisition, he would lose the key staff who had made Fore worth the price he had paid for it. And some did leave, rather too quickly for Simpson's comfort. This was a world of skill shortages: the industry was growing so fast that there were not enough highly qualified people to go around.

'The biggest problem this industry has got is people,' said Meakin. 'It's a huge, fast-growing, exciting, dynamic industry – ironically just like the car industry used to be.' The Marconi team knew that it had to make the company attractive enough to ensure that the trickle of departures from Fore did not turn into a flood. Part of the answer, of course, was through pay packages and incentives – in particular the incentive of stock options.

Those options could not exist in a vacuum: they had to be underpinned by evidence that the group was going places that would take the share price up with it. In short, Marconi had to perform. To do that, it had to attract and retain high-quality people by ensuring that they felt fulfilled in their work, while from the company's standpoint fulfilling their potential to help drive the group forward.

In Marconi's quest to create this virtuous circle, Meakin's partnership with WMG assumed a dual and crucial significance. Meakin said: 'What you have to do is get the right quality people, get a sense of belonging and ownership and commitment to what the organisation is trying to achieve. It's like seedlings: you've got to give them space and light and water and let them grow.

'That, essentially, is the transfer to Marconi. The old GEC parts of the business don't have that type of background. The new parts that we bought have always lived with that part of the world. We are trying to bring this together.' Under the new learning partnership, WMG would cement this corporate culture change. And the Fore purchase, while making WMG's role all the more vital for the company, also greatly extended Warwick's scope for action and the resources of know-how that it could access.

Clive Reynolds, one of the WMG men running the Marconi partnership, said: 'When we started working with them [Marconi], they were still GEC and over half the company was still defence business. The vision was the same as it is today: to introduce a genuinely global programme to make a genuinely global company. But during the course of 1999, as they changed themselves into a global telecoms and IT company, it all became more apposite. We needed a US partner. They bought Reltec and Fore.'

Fore's close links with Carnegie Mellon carried WMG into the heart of the internet revolution. Apart from spawning Fore, the Pittsburgh university had also given birth to Lycos, one of the original web search engines. Bhattacharyya was already well advanced in his thinking about how to re-engineer WMG for e-business education and technological development. He had put out feelers to the Massachusetts Institute of Technology (MIT) about forging a transatlantic link, but without any firm result. Now Carnegie Mellon promised to fill that gap, enabling WMG to develop its own ideas while accessing leading-edge American thinking.

Specifically and immediately, the Carnegie Mellon connection gave WMG's partnership with Marconi the American academic base it needed to deliver the programme transatlantically.

Meakin and Warwick had already decided that they needed a full-scale master's degree course, which had to be taught on either side of the Atlantic. 'Carnegie Mellon was not an easy choice,' said Reynolds. 'But it was a fairly natural choice because of their links with software and e-business. The people who created Fore came from Carnegie Mellon. So Rob Meakin's vision of a master's that made a difference to the company, as opposed to the individual, coincided with the building blocks coming in to make that vision a reality.'

When Marconi bought Fore, Bhattacharyya's team and Meakin were already well advanced in their thinking about the form and substance of the partnership programme. The prime objective was clear: Meakin had concluded that Marconi needed to attract about 400 top-quality graduates a year from around the world. They would provide the sustained influx of new blood needed to build the new group. 'You don't change an organisation's culture just by changing its name,' said Tim Bridgeman, director of WMG's education programmes. 'And there is the huge middle level of management that they have to take with them. There is an urgency: Marconi is targeting telecoms and information technology, so the organisation has to be more fleet of foot.'

But Marconi had a perception problem to overcome. Bridgeman said: 'The truth is, if you were a top-quality electronics engineer, why would you have wanted to go and work for GEC?' Although GEC was renowned for its technology, like most technology groups, it had problems with graduate retention. 'Technology graduates find the realities of the world of work rather challenging. You therefore see high graduate turnover during a two-to-three-year period,' Bridgeman said. One basic aim of the development programme was therefore clear: to ensure Marconi attracted the high-quality graduates it needed, and to keep them tied in during the first few years of employment.

To meet their goals, Meakin and Bhattacharyya's team decided to create a Marconi MSc in International Technology, which would be offered to every graduate the company recruited, wherever that was in the world, subject only to the performance of the individual concerned since he or she joined Marconi.

Meakin believed the degree-level qualification was vital, both to fulfil the personal development ambitions of the graduates who took the course, and to satisfy Marconi's aim of enhancing the quality of its future managers. 'I thought it was important to have a goal,' Meakin believed. 'Having an MSc at the end of it gave people an extra incentive to undertake the course.'

Bridgeman agreed: 'Being told that you are in a recruitment process and will be enrolled in a world-class technology management master's programme is a real carrot,' he said. The format should also aid retention: 'You will have the same problem at twenty-six/twenty-seven that you now have at twenty-three/ twenty-four,' he said. 'But at the later ages, these people will be going into senior positions, especially if the company has been able to identify the really good ones, which is difficult to do at twenty-four when you have only had two or three years of graduate development.'

Meakin and the WMG team aimed high. They wanted to build the programme to the point where 200 graduates on either side of the Atlantic were taking the course each year. The minimum aim was to reach a first base where 100 were going through in both Europe and Pittsburgh. 'If we don't get those numbers, we won't be able to achieve the international best-in-class programme standard,' Bridgeman said in spring 2000. 'I would like it to be 200 a year to justify the immense organisational issues we have to put behind this to make it work.'

If the scale of the programme was ambitious, its design was truly radical. It was aimed at giving Marconi's graduates access to the best thinking available. Like the leader of a big industrial project, Warwick was appointed as prime contractor, but in terms of pure delivery, Warwick would account for only about 25 per cent of the modular programme.

The rest was to be provided by a galaxy of technology management talent at other leading universities: Cambridge, with which Marconi had also forged a research link, Imperial College, University College London (UCL), Southampton and Parma in Europe, together with Carnegie Mellon in the US. In all, about twelve universities would be involved. 'It is quite difficult to go anywhere and get that level of teaching woven into the same programme,' said Meakin.

In Europe, Warwick was to award the degree; in America, Carnegie Mellon would be the accrediting institution. Both distance learning and residential courses were to be used. 'I wanted to try and offer our people the opportunity to benefit from the best teaching that we could get anywhere around the world,' Meakin said. 'But I didn't want them to have to go to it; I wanted to bring the teaching to them.'

175

The concept required academic pride and ego to be sublimated to the overall purpose of the venture. From the outset, there was recognition at both Warwick and in the other participating institutions that they needed each other to make the programme work. Bridgeman said: 'Bringing together educational resource is something we are experienced in. But trying to get your peers on the international stage to work with you is very difficult, because they are bound to ask what's in it for them.

'We will be awarding a University of Warwick degree, but as a premier division university, we are recognising that we can't actually be a world-class player in every technology. That's a very difficult thing to admit, but it is a fact that you need to go to UCL for systems integration expertise, or Southampton for photonics.'

It was pioneering work. Part of the reason was that, because Marconi was now operating at the leading edge of communications technology, the programmes to educate graduates in this area of expertise simply did not exist. Like the manufacturer who has to design a new die in order to make an innovative product, Marconi and WMG had to invent a format that would deliver what they needed.

Similarly, Marconi was both developing new networking products and using that technology inside its own organisation. That also had implications for the design of the course, which had to face both outwards and inwards. 'If you look at the technology and think e-commerce, then Marconi makes the integrated systems but also has to use them to run its own business, so it matters to both Marconi and its customers,' said Reynolds. 'This made course design difficult: it's not just training; you have to give some brainpower too.'

'We have no benchmarks,' Bridgeman said. 'These programmes just do not exist. Students will probably go to more than seven different institutions to do their degree, and they are unlikely to do more than two or three modules at any one university. This is a very, very different approach from anything that has been tried before.'

Bridgeman believed that it would be a trailblazer for industry–university collaboration in management education. 'It is a very interesting template for how industrially focused programmes are delivered in the future,' he said. 'WMG is the systems integrator, the organisation that makes sense of the whole programme, puts it in a framework and, at the end of the day, pulls it all together to produce an educational qualification.

'We are only dealing with other premier universities, and the prime reason they will be selected is because they are considered by the industry to be state of the art. But that means we can deliver a truly international, best-in-class programme. It's not easy or cheap, but if that's what you set out to do, because you are not pulling it all in in-house, you don't have to compromise.'

The e-business world permeated the course environment. 'We are making the whole programme mirror the idea of e-business,' said Reynolds. One third of the work is spent in groups working on a pseudo-internet. Students conduct internet scenario planning, then test their assumptions. 'We have created a website [Marconi-.com/masters] for them to check or challenge their assumptions,' said Reynolds. 'We will create virtual assets and simulate the way the assets are operated. The students will tell us today what sort of company we should create for tomorrow.'

E-business technology was not only the central component of course content, it was instrumental in delivering the programme. The first thirty-eight graduates, who arrived at Warwick for induction in September 1999, were addressed over a live video-conferencing link with Pittsburgh by Steve Schmidt, one of Fore's founders. Then they headed for Cambridge, where they started work on their first module.

'We are using enabling technologies to deliver the course modules,' said Bridgeman. 'The web is being used to source all our material, and to extend past the module to create virtual teaching teams. They may have returned to the US, Italy or another part of the UK, but they are still working as a team in post-module activity, using the internet.'

The second group, of forty graduates, started at Warwick in March 2000, with the first Carnegie Mellon course opening the following month. To ensure continuity and uniformity on either side of the Atlantic, Warwick and Carnegie Mellon swapped teaching, with WMG delivering some software modules for Carnegie Mellon, and vice versa. Live video-conferencing links with Carnegie Mellon were an integral part of the course.

WMG brought the expertise it had developed during its work with AstraZeneca and BAE to the Marconi programme. The difference was that this was the first time it had applied such experience at the level of a master's course. 'There are learning objectives, performance objectives,' Reynolds said. 'Participants are expected to have learning contracts with their line managers.'

There were other new departures. 'Our first module had to be very ambitious – a ground-breaking module,' said Reynolds. The course contained a much higher technology element than WMG's traditional engineering business management programmes. Because of the company–university partnership approach, issues of which modules were core and which optional were more highly charged than usual.

Reynolds said: 'The development process was very tricky because one of Marconi's requirements was that this should be a proper consortium of international providers, and that decisions must be joint. It was not a question of Marconi insisting on something or Warwick deciding.'

The programme again highlighted the divergence of the Warwick Way from the conventional MBA approach. 'You don't take a syllabus and foist it on the students,' said Reynolds. 'The heart of it has to be very sound. It is based on academic learning principles, but at the same time it has to be enterprising. So we consulted with both engineering and non-engineering managers on what practical subject areas they needed to cover. There were only two strategy subjects to start because we weren't being pseudo-MBA. This was about twenty-seven-year-olds in the engine room.'

Meakin was delighted with the initial response, which he said was distinguished by 'huge enthusiasm' and 'really good reports' from the participants. But he was already working with Bhattacharyya to strengthen his technology education drive.

In September 2000, the first twenty students arrived at Warwick for the inaugural Marconi three-year undergraduate degree course in Telecommunications Technology. They were eighteen-year-old school-leavers who had been hired by the company, and would spend two-thirds of their time inside Marconi and one third at the university.

The course evoked the partnership degree concept that Meakin and Bhattacharyya had developed at Rover. 'Their experience in the company, the job they will do and the training they will receive is all designed hand-in-glove with Warwick,' Meakin said. 'At the end of the day, the student will obtain a degree from a great university, fully transportable so that people can get up and go if they want, although they are more likely to stay with us.'

The aim was to develop suitably qualified people to improve performance in the mid-levels of the business – an area of competitiveness where UK plc is conspicuously weak compared with most of its rivals. Meakin and Bhattacharyya were originally inspired by the old technician apprentice scheme which had fallen into disuse in British industry. 'To attract the same calibre of young person now, you have to be offering a degree-type qualification,' said Meakin. 'We are learning from our experience in Rover and BAE. We want to improve the intake of qualified young people at the bottom of the business.'

Meakin expected most of the students to be from local families in the Coventry area, and that the introduction of university tuition fees would enhance the attraction of the Marconi degree course. Meakin said: 'The other fundamental attraction for us is that, this way, we can combat the fact that there are fewer and fewer young people taking the subjects that make them suitable candidates for the sort of degrees which are the lifeblood of this industry.'

Faced with this dearth of science and maths students, Meakin and Bhattacharyya agreed that Marconi should aim to tap into the A-level students who were studying arts or languages. All of them were now skilled in the use of personal computers and information technology, so the foundations on which the undergraduate degree course could build were there.

'Young people are forced to specialise at an early stage,' said Meakin. 'If we get to them earlier, while they still have a breadth of interests, we can try to attract them to our type of work. When they get into it, they love it.'

But Meakin and Bhattacharyya knew they could go still further. In late 2000, they were considering a venture that would take the partnership degree principle still deeper into the heart of the formative process of education for industry. 'The real challenge for us is whether we can take the three-year degree and turn it into a five-year degree with sixteen-year-olds participating,' Meakin said. 'If we can get to that, we will have opened up a huge new range of people.'

Their deliberations had not gone far when Marconi was engulfed in a crisis that threatened its entire existence. Early in 2001, the American telecoms equipment boom turned to bust. The speed and scale of the decline was unprecedented in the young industry's short history, sweeping up all the players, large and small. Nortel was forced into a $19.1 billion write-off; Lucent, once the industry leader, teetered on the edge of bankruptcy; JDS Uniphase, which specialised in optical transmission technology, suffered one of the highest losses in corporate history. Even Cisco, the darling of Wall Street, endured a share price collapse.

As one of the smaller players, Marconi was more vulnerable than most. As its sales slumped and profits evaporated, its share price melted down – touching 12p at one point in the autumn. Investor confidence in the top management collapsed: within a few months, both Mayo and Simpson left, together with Sir Roger Hurn, the chairman. Derek Bonham, the steely former Hanson finance director, took the chair; Mike Parton became chief executive. They wrote off the entire acquisition cost of Fore, whose market had been particularly hard hit by the US slump. Meakin resigned from the group in March 2002. By then, the company still had a long, long way to go before securing its survival.

The crisis did not invalidate Bhattacharyya's work. Instead, it added urgency to the management education drive. The skills that WMG had been aiming to inculcate into the company were now even more critical to its future than they had been previously. Either that knowledge would be used to revive Marconi's fortunes as an independent entity, or – much more likely – it would help reserve enough value to encourage a bigger player to buy the business – or what was left of it.

Above all, despite the company's travails, in an educative context the Marconi collaboration had proved its worth as a testbed for Bhattacharyya's biggest project since he had founded WMG. Using what he dubbed E2 – electronic engineering business management – he planned to re-engineer Warwick so that it would be in the forefront of the early twenty-first century internet revolution.

Chapter Nine
E2 – The Net Generation

At the heart of Kumar Bhattacharyya's expanded International Manufacturing Centre is a new concept of management education for the internet age. Bhattacharyya calls it E2 – electronic engineering business management. It is the vehicle through which Warwick will help its clients harness the potential of electronic business to transform their competitiveness.

The application of E2 to education and product and process development will be the specific centrepiece of the second phase of the IMC, which opened its doors in 2002. More generally, E2 will influence Warwick's whole approach to technology education and development as the group enters its third decade of growth. 'This is a huge change in the industrial landscape,' Bhattacharyya said in late 2001. 'We need to change as well, in order to stay at the leading edge.'

Unlike the many people who caught dotcom fever at the turn of the nineties, Bhattacharyya never subscribed to the view that the net rendered existing business models obsolete. Nor did he believe, despite the initial mania for e-tail companies, that the net's greatest impact would be in the business-to-consumer area. To Bhattacharyya, it was clear that the staying power of the internet would be in business-to-business applications.

He saw the net as part of the information technology continuum that dated back to the first widespread use of computers in business in the early 1960s. But he also recognised that the net was a dramatic development of that continuum – it created a springboard for a quantum leap forward in the use of IT in business management. 'If you assume that the world changed one million times since the start of the computer age, then this will be change on a scale of one billion times,' he said.

Just as the internet itself was a landmark in the use of IT to improve competitiveness, so Bhattacharyya's concept of E2 fell naturally, albeit dramatically, into the evolution of WMG. Bhattacharyya traced a line back to the group's *raison d'être*, his analysis of British industry's weaknesses, and its early emphasis on computer-aided design and manufacture (Cad/Cam) as a partial remedy.

'We realised early on that British industry had a fundamental weakness in the field of design – design for engineering and manufacturing. On top of that, the general approach was to adopt management systems using big computers, big IT. But that led to the creation of large computer sections in companies which were separate from other departments such as engineering. There was a yawning gulf between the computer department and others. IT was not user-friendly – there was no proper network inside companies, or between customers and suppliers; their cost base was high. Technological integration just wasn't there.

'Initially, when we tried to deal with the supply base, trying to achieve this integration was a horrendous task. Cad/Cam helped us a lot, but even with that we were still in a quite imperfect situation. So the migration to e-commerce came very naturally to us. That was always going to be the solution to the IT management integration issue. When it became economic, when the internet came into being and the network started building, we went straight for e-commerce in a really big way.'

Crucially, Bhattacharyya had two important relationships in place that facilitated the re-orientation of WMG. One was with Sun Microsystems, the specialist workstation and networking company for designers and engineers, which had withstood the challenge of the Microsoft/Intel alliance. Sun had established four manufacturing centres of excellence in the Western world: two in the US – in San Diego and Philadelphia – one in the Netherlands, and one, Semcoe, at WMG. Three of the centres were operated with an industrial collaborator; Semcoe – the Sun European Manufacturing Centre of Excellence – at Warwick was Sun's only academic partner. WMG's other key partnership was with the American group Parametric Technology Corporation (PTC), a world leader in the design and development of Cad/Cam systems for industries such as engineering and aerospace, which owed its prominence partly to the 1997 acquisition of a then-rival, Computervision.

Warwick had a long-standing partnership with Computervision which had been sealed by Sandy Moffat in the late 1980s. Initially, Computervision – like other original equipment producers at the time – carried out training on their home site in Basingstoke. After a while, the Americans began to send overflow customers to WMG for training on the software, and soon more and more companies started asking to come to Warwick, because of its facilities. WMG and the Americans then signed a mutually beneficial contract: 'We entered into a dialogue with Computervision,' Moffat recalled. 'We said, "You are a software company interested in selling your product; you aren't necessarily very good at training people. It would make more sense if you were connected with people who were professional trainers, who could deliver that on your behalf."' The deal was done. 'They continued to front with the customer; we delivered the training. It was very successful,' Moffat said.

By the early nineties, however, WMG was looking to expand its role. 'We developed from simply being a mechanism for the delivery of training to one which wanted to develop the training courses to be more appropriate to the UK market,' Moffat said. 'Until then, we had prepared courses provided by Computervision US. Their business drivers were somewhat different, so the courses were not set up for UK practice. For a start, they were long. In the US, it would be nonsense to fly someone from one side of the country to the other for a two-day course. In Britain, two-day courses were preferred by many customers.'

Computervision acceded to Warwick's suggestion that the group should customise the software packages for the UK market. First, WMG asked customers what they would prefer. Shorter courses than in the US dictated that the course content should be different, too. 'Rather than teaching people the activities associated with a particular software model, we modularised the software so that it was divided between, say, surface modelling and solid modelling. That still necessitated week-long courses, though. So we broke it down further, so that it could be made bespoke and could enable people to learn their job without the frilly bits,' said Moffat. A five-day instruction in solid modelling thus became a manageable two-day course.

Once inside the customer for the first time, new points-of-departure avenues appeared for WMG. At Rover, British Aerospace and VSEL, the Barrow-based nuclear submarine builder, WMG staff met engineers who asked them to go beyond basic Cad/Cam training to advising how to integrate the new software into the whole engineering process. 'It was an evolution,' Moffat said. It also opened WMG's eyes to the potential in mainland Europe.

'In Italy, France, Germany, everyone was taking these US-type courses. In France, people were modifying them for French, but that was about as far as it went,' said Moffat. 'We established the Computervision European University at Warwick to make these concepts available throughout Europe.' WMG developed the course materials and established training centres in Milan, Wiesbaden, Munich and Paris.

'The idea was to try and centralise the development process, to make it more akin to a European way of thinking,' said Moffat. 'We pushed down to project manager level. The principles were: reduce the size of courses, make them more marketable, more attractive, closer to customer needs. That worked very well. It was a different way of operating; we weren't just regurgitating something from a book.' The deal with Computervision was worth $40m over four years.

The relationship went further, both geographically and in depth. WMG opened a training centre within its Hong Kong operation. It took on a project for Computervision in Singapore – Moffat was seconded to the US company for two years to work on that. Computervision also took Warwick into the US. 'We were instrumental in helping Hughes Space and Communications [at the time, General Motors' aerospace arm] in the development of their Cad/Cam/electronic data management strategy,' said Moffat. The expertise was also applied to existing WMG clients, notably BAE and Rover, including the car-maker's period under BMW ownership. 'We worked on the Freelander, the Rover 75 and the Mini. As a result, we saw Mini on the computer screen in its finished, assembled form before many others. That was one of our finest moments, I think,' said Moffat.

The Computervision link provided the software element in WMG's pioneering design and engineering education effort. The Sun connection, which developed contemporaneously, provided the hardware expertise that WMG also needed.

Warwick's connection with Sun eventually led the group into areas at the leading edge of digital engineering design. But it originated in a classic case of Bhattacharyya commercial pragmatism. WMG's first contact with Sun came in 1992, when the American group donated some workstations to help support the group's development work. The contact was renewed by Vinesh Raja, one of Bhattacharyya's longest-standing colleagues and an expert in manufacturing systems simulation, when the International Manufacturing Centre (IMC) was conceived in 1994. 'We were going to put the IMC up and I was tasked to source equipment for the building,' Raja recalled. 'The strategy was to try and source the equipment on a partnership basis, not on a customer/supplier basis.'

Bhattacharyya and Raja invited Sun to participate in the IMC venture. Other industrial partners were being recruited, with the objective of ensuring that when phase one of the IMC was completed in 1995, the building would be fully equipped through such collaborative deals. 'That was the Professor's decision,' said Raja. 'He knew that when you buy equipment, it goes out of date in six months or a year. So in order to stay at the leading edge, you face the ongoing cost of replacing the equipment, a cost which the university would have struggled to meet. He knew that there would come a time when the university would not be able to afford this kind of equipment.'

Raja knew he faced a difficult job. 'You could knock on people's doors and ask for equipment, but we didn't have a building – all I had was an artist's impression. The concept was so novel that it made it very difficult to ask whether the company wanted to be a partner. I met quite a lot of good people, but many pointed me to the door. Others said they were interested in principle – but how many interesteds do you convert into reality?'

Even though WMG had by now been operating for almost fifteen years, Raja found it hard to overcome the credibility gap. Bhattacharyya's concept was for a centre where WMG staff and clients would work side by side on commercially relevant applications that improved competitiveness, including robotics, automation and logistics, as well as more thematic areas such as design, innovation, supply chain management and partnerships with small and medium-sized enterprises. Many of the companies Raja contacted could not associate this concept, so different from a blue-sky research laboratory, with a university.

'It was difficult for some companies to grasp that we were part of an academic institution, yet the work we were doing was directly related to engineering businesses,' said Raja. 'They saw universities as academic institutions who didn't care about students when they left here. I told them that we liked to train people who were more useful to industry.'

In the end, he got the message across to enough companies. Two large machine tool makers saw the light: the American-owned Cincinatti Milacron and Bridgport-Grundy. Milacron was already a WMG partner; Bridgport was new to Warwick, and required a good deal of persuasion. Bhattacharyya's emphasis on recruiting senior staff from industry's front line, rather than from academia's back room, unlocked the door. Bridgport's managing director was won over when Raja, a machine tools expert, demonstrated that he knew what he was talking about. The MD realised that the company's investment in the IMC would be put to good use by good hands. 'The IMC experience was not going to be a question of pure maths,' said Raja. 'You aren't talking thermodynamics here. It is about setting things up on the machine; it's about working in an operational, not an experimental, environment.'

By the time the IMC opened for business, it contained enough high-tech equipment to be the envy of any company's engineering centre. There were three- and four-axis computer numerically-controlled (CNC) machines; a CNC-controlled co-ordinated meas-uring machine; an assembly cell; lasers and other CNC machine tools; automated storage systems and an automated self-guided vehicle (AGV). It also contained a significant amount of Sun equipment. That did not come easily. Of all the partnership deals, the Sun contract was the hardest for Raja to reach.

'It took ages to secure their agreement,' said Raja. 'They were interested in the idea, because they were planning to build up a very strong presence in Cad/Cam hardware. At first, I talked to

Sun in the UK about our manufacturing focus. They began to realise that this had some good potential. I was also helped by a coincidence: Sun in America had just recruited someone in marketing for manufacturing. They formed an alliance with a Cad/ Cam company who also sold the hardware on their behalf – so Sun had very rarely been to see a client itself. Then, when some of the Cad vendors started supplying multiple platforms, Sun had to go and sell their kit themselves. They had to go through a very big, very fast learning curve to ensure they maintained their market share.'

The Sun people could see the attractions of establishing a working showcase for their engineering and manufacturing net-works within Bhattacharyya's IMC. But investment in Warwick was a strategic decision, taken from the top. 'They sent twelve to fifteen Americans here for a day to look at our place and discuss with us what our vision was and what they should be doing,' said Raja. 'We told them that we were not there to dictate what they should be doing, but simply to talk about what we thought was likely to happen in the world. On the back of that, they could decide how they should run their business.'

Sun was convinced. A multi-million-pound partnership with WMG was signed and Semcoe was born, specialising in IT applications for manufacturers. It rapidly became a powerhouse within the IMC powerhouse. 'The basic idea was to work with manufacturing companies, to explain to them why IT was very important to them, and, above all, to show them practically how IT can help manufacturers. Semcoe allowed them to try things out hands-on, to come and see IT systems for themselves,' said Raja.

One important stream of Semcoe's activity was to develop ways of integrating Cad/Cam with Enterprise Resource Planning (ERP) and EDM – Moffat's Engineering Data Management. WMG and Sun soon found a client who wanted to run a pilot project. The environment concerned could not have been more critical: the customer was VSEL, the Barrow-based shipbuilder which was also using Computervision software. And the particular project related to the Batch 2 Trafalgar-class nuclear hunter-killer submarines, which had been recently ordered by the Ministry of Defence.

For its architecture, Semcoe pioneered the use in a manufacturing context of 'object-based integration', a system used in financial dealing rooms. It is an ethernet-based system overlaid by a software 'bus'. The various applications required were connected to the software bus through a box – 'the box of tricks', Raja called it. The set-up meant that, on an EDM application such as releasing bills of material, the box would package those bills in object form before launching them on to the bus – the act of 'publishing' the bills. An ERP user could then subscribe to this information, and the receiving box would convert the object-based bills of material to a native format.

'This method had a lot of advantages over the conventional networking system,' said Raja. 'Normally, people were doing point-to-point integration, where you have two systems and build a link between them. Then you add another system and another. The problem is that the larger the number of systems you have, the more complex the integrated network becomes. Point-to-point interfaces are quite complex, and when one of those systems changes, you cannot just change one link – you have to change all the links associated with that particular application.

'That led to a lot of manufacturing companies either having large IT departments or contracting out their IT operations at significant cost. The method we developed allows companies to control things with a very small number of IT staff, or to considerably reduce the amount of out-sourced work. The system won't overload your ethernet either.' It also had a guaranteed delivery system, so that if someone was away for a week, he or she could kick off the system when they returned to work and find an old version of a document, if they needed one.

'We were the first to pilot these ideas in manufacturing,' said Raja. 'The system is quite commonly used in the finance industry, where trading houses use it to deal in money at very high speeds to the third or fourth decimal place. The difference between a trading house and a manufacturer is that in the City, when you talk bills of materials, they are several megabytes in size — you aren't just changing one number. And, unlike a dealer, the manufacturer does not need his bills of material to be updated every nanosecond — then you'd never be able to change anything because it would be changing so fast.'

Tailored to VSEL's needs, the system worked smoothly and delivered precisely what was wanted. 'We had no traffic problems,' said Raja. 'Packet collision — when you send something and it can't get there because it can't be identified — is a danger in any system, but that wasn't a major problem at all in this.' So impressed was GEC, then VSEL's owner, that it planned to run a large pilot within twenty companies through the group, with custom-designed modifications to suit each subsidiary.

WMG's existing industry relationships helped Semcoe to make significant advances with automotive and aerospace groups in the field of reverse-engineering new products. Clay modelling is used throughout those and other engineering industries, by both original equipment manufacturers and component suppliers, to produce a physical model of the product or part. In the case of a new car, up to seven full-size 'clays' may be made at different stages of the product's development.

'Our reverse-engineering technique will digitally scan the physical model and make another model, which becomes your master model,' said Raja. 'The idea of reverse-engineering is not to replace the clays, but to replace and reduce the number of clays needed. That's good for any product — car, vacuum cleaner or hair drier. It's not good enough just to do this on a computer — engineers are guys who like to touch and feel. What we are doing is using IT to improve the traditional process.'

In aerospace, Semcoe investigated how to move to rapid production of high-integrity components with partners including

BAE, GKN, TRW – which bought Lucas in 1999 – the Aeromet casting company and Bridgport. 'We studied high-speed machining and rapid prototyping for producing a component, or for producing a tool to make that component,' said Raja. 'Volumes in aerospace are very small, so sometimes tooling by forging is not appropriate because the cost is enormous. So we looked at high-speed milling, which can cut at several metres a minute. There is a lot of R&D work involved with this.'

By the turn of the century, Semcoe had been operating for more than five years and the partners were looking at its next phase. This was likely to lead to refinement of the structure, with the generic centre being divided and segmented into centres of excellence dedicated to particular industries. 'An automotive centre of excellence would focus on all aspects of using IT to enhance your processes,' said Raja. 'It would look at how to provide all the tool stores needed by engineers to work on vehicle design and development, from styling to manufacturing. It would also focus on the whole supply chain, from second- and third-tier component makers at one end to dealers at the other.'

Semcoe's work ran concurrently and complementarily with that of Moffat on the Cad/Cam software side. Here, too, by 2001 WMG was probing deeper into supply chain development. 'Globally, the business drivers are changing fairly significantly,' said Moffat. 'The old drivers, such as price and quality, are no longer paramount. Consumers take them for granted. If you have £15,000 now and want to buy a car, you have a myriad of choices. You wouldn't expect to pay a lot more for any of the vehicles in that category, and you would expect similar levels of quality in all of them.

'Branding is quite important in the choice, but what makes a strong brand? People now are driven more by choice and speed of response – which in the car industry means delivery. I want to buy a BMW with particular wheels and colour. When can I have it? If I can get exactly what I want when I want it, which is quickly, I will support that brand and I will probably be prepared to pay a premium for my car.'

The need to create or reinforce that virtuous circle was recognised by premium car-makers. That was why, in the early twenty-first century, they were placing huge emphasis on streamlining the entire supply pipeline, from design studio to showroom. 'Companies are reducing their inventories, becoming tighter and leaner and more switched on,' said Moffat. 'Before, their attitude was: "This is what you need; who wants to buy it?" Now it's a question of: "What do you want to buy when? We'll see if we can achieve that."'

In the drive to truncate each stage of the supply pipeline, improved data flow – in terms of both speed and accuracy – was critical. 'To stay with that market-leading edge, companies have to look at how they can deliver greater choice to the consumer, but in the shortest possible time,' said Moffat. 'This is where the importance of concurrent engineering comes in.'

The notion of concurrent engineering – originally called simultaneous engineering – developed during the 1990s. It grew out of the lean manufacturing ideology, and from the same source: Japan. Western manufacturers in industries such as automotive tried to abandon the traditional linear method of product development, in which the designers handed on to the product engineers who handed over to the production engineers and so on. Instead, they sought to compress the time to market by deploying multi-disciplinary teams of engineers from different departments. These teams would work simultaneously, or concurrently, to iron out problems and develop products that, would come closer to meeting consumer demand and be capable of high-quality, fault-free manufacture.

The move to concurrent engineering was generally successful. It facilitated significant rethinking of the manufacturing process, triggering the trend by OEMs, (original equipment manufacturers) to focus on assembly and to delegate increasing responsibility for the design and development of large sub-systems to first-tier suppliers. By the early twenty-first century, however, manufacturers – aware now of what was possible – were seeking still greater pace and precision in concurrent engineering in order to capture that potential. 'Formula One has adopted concurrent engineering for many years, but it is a relatively small operation, usually based on one site,' said Moffat. 'Whereas Airbus is a global operation with main sites and support sites all over the place. How do you bring these all together? The answer is engineering data management.'

WMG's relationship with Parametric positioned the group to be among the world front-runners in developing engineering data management (EDM). In the late 1990s, Warwick and PTC co-operated in the development of Gold Optegra, a first-generation engineering data management system for Airbus. 'EDM is a toolbox,' said Moffat. 'It was derived from Cad/Cam. It is emerging now like Cad/Cam did in the early eighties. It is a dynamic working system that creates a very specific audit trail. It provides greater manufacturing flexibility, greater choice, shorter lead times. It is a crucial tool for companies to meet customer needs at the most competitive possible price.

'With EDM, you are able to create data. You can then store that data in a virtual vault. The vault is like a large bucket of information and on to that you assign attributes relating to a particular development project, such as an engine or a car. The vault can be accessed by anybody in the virtual environment with the necessary clearance, so that everyone in the company has access in real time to all the information appropriate to that project. In Optegra, there were distributed vaults at Filton, in Aérospatiale in France and in Dasa in Germany. Every now and then, people reading that data would phone each other to discuss it.'

Springboarding off the Optegra experience, Warwick and PTC launched into EDM work on a number of fronts. Moffat said: 'An EDM environment allows you to see the whole product – you can watch an aircraft or car being built virtually and know exactly where and when to make your contribution. This is the definition of IT: delivering the right information to the right people at the right time.'

Some of Warwick's work is aimed at helping companies overcome the difficulties of applying EDM. 'EDM is constructed around your process and is relatively easy to use, but it's quite difficult to customise in a form that's relevant to your company,' Moffat said. 'A lot of companies are struggling with this type of technology, because they are missing a trick. All they are doing is speeding up an old process, so they are finding that things are running into each other quicker.' The result is an IT traffic jam. 'People need to stand back and get their manufacturing system right, get the proper new tools in.'

From his vantage point, Vinesh Raja was delivering the same message about business process re-engineering to capitalise on the opportunities created by the internet revolution. 'Everyone is so focused now on IT that they don't focus on the business,' said Raja. 'IT should never drive a company's management; management must drive the IT. In the first instance, companies need to de-couple IT from business. They need to go away from it in order to come back more informed. Once they have done that, and worked out what they need from IT to enhance their company's competitiveness, then they can start looking at IT again in a more relevant way,' he said.

But from Bhattacharyya down, senior Warwick executives were united in their view of the efficiency-transforming power of the internet. 'We are on the edge of the information age,' Moffat said in late 2001. 'It is quite difficult to understand what that means, because this is the equivalent of the immediate pre-industrialisation age almost three centuries ago.' But the internet would have a wide-reaching impact on Warwick and its clients: 'The information age will push us towards training given in very small modularised chunks. It will be done interactively, and ultimately across the net.

Assessment of people's performance will also be done across the net. Today, it's very difficult to assess an individual objectively. Whether you think they are adding value or not depends on a subjective view of the business.'

It was a reflection of the entrepreneurial culture with which Bhattacharyya had imbued WMG that the organisation viewed the net as a huge opportunity, both for itself and for its customers. To Bhattacharyya and his colleagues, the internet revolution was an enormous catalyst for the application of the principles and practices that had powered WMG's growth. 'We were ahead of the game because of the way we had worked with Cad and integrated systems for many years,' he said. 'From the early 1990s, we were forging links in both directions, vertically into schools and horizontally into companies, so that we would be in the forefront of the revolution we could see coming.'

One venture did more than any other single initiative to establish WMG in the forefront of schools education for the IT age. It was the product of a conversation one day in 1998 in the Houses of Parliament between Bhattacharyya and PTC's two top executives, Steve Walske and Barry Cohen. 'Kumar said that if PTC really wanted to show a European audience that we were a world-class company, then we had to do something that both demonstrated our technological leadership and related it to the domestic community,' Cohen recalled.

The result was a ground-breaking £20m WMG–PTC programme to distribute the American group's design software to all Britain's 6,000 secondary schools in a rolling programme covering between 500 and 600 schools a year. The Software in Schools deal was welcomed by the Blair government as a means of taking the then-current Cad/Cam element of the National Curriculum to a new level. Many educationists were sceptical, both about the partners' ability to disseminate the software and about the efficacy of the material should it get through to design departments.

But, as sixteen boys and five girls at George Ward School in

Melksham near Avon, demonstrated in 2000, the doubters were proved wrong. Using PTC's software in a competition sponsored by BAE, the class of sixteen-year olds designed a new supersonic jetliner that would travel above the atmosphere for maximum speed. The GCSE students worked with pupils from five other schools to develop the idea for the competition, which attracted fifty-five schools from six different regional groups. Tony Booth, George Ward's design and technology advanced skills teacher, said the project had helped enthuse the teenagers about design for industry: 'The children have been hugely motivated,' he said. 'In education, we have to be as smart as industry; if we aren't, you cannot expect young people to get excited about industry.' Bhattacharyya remained confident about the future: 'Large numbers of children are now getting excited about industrial design, thanks to Software in Schools. That can only help engineering and the British economy.'

With its track record of involvement in IT education at all levels, from schoolroom to corporate head office, WMG approached the e-business revolution from a position of confidence and, Bhattacharyya believed, strength: 'We could see this coming, and we realised that there was no way a university could reinvent itself suddenly by saying, "Right, now let's get into e-commerce." In order to enter the field authoritatively, you had to understand where the industrial sector was coming from.'

But the huge opportunity presented by the demand for e-business management skills still had to be grasped. And to grasp it, WMG itself had to be re-engineered.

It took two years for Bhattacharyya and his team to reposition WMG for the internet age with E2, Electronic Engineering Business Management. When the internet explosion began in the late 1990s, Bhattacharyya was already familiar with the net because of its use by academic institutions. An intranet already operated in WMG. Warwick staff tracked the net's increasing application to the business world. They observed Warwick's first principle: listening to its customers. WMG analysed the attitude to the internet of its industrial clients, which by now numbered about 500 worldwide. The conclusion was clear: huge demand was building up to harness the business improvement potential of the net, but there was widespread ignorance of how to convert that potential into actual management practice.

The findings reinforced Bhattacharyya's convictions about the internet. Its principle significance, he said, was at last to make or bring closer to working reality notions – such as the virtual company, home-working and the paperless office – that had existed for a decade and more. 'For the first time, people will be managing businesses entirely electronically,' he said. The fundamental challenge was to modernise both the forms and the content of business education so that individuals were better equipped to realise – in both senses of that word – what the net made possible. 'Revolutions have never changed any organisation,' Bhattacharyya observed. 'They just cause huge hiccups. E-commerce alone doesn't do anything or solve anything. You have to have the skill base to exploit it. It is easy to confuse e-commerce and e-management. People think you can make decisions without possessing or understanding the necessary decision-making tools.'

By the same token, managers armed with those tools would find that the net made it possible to capture vast efficiency benefits. 'The internet allows you to simplify management,' Bhattacharyya said. 'Therefore, you can reduce overhead costs by a very large amount and dramatically accelerate your speed of movement. The internet brings transparency and precision. It makes tools available that allow you to develop things in parallel. That makes decision implementation much easier and the chances of success much higher. Whoever seizes this opportunity first will have a time advantage over their competitors. With the internet, you are now talking real IT. It allows data capture at an unprecedented speed and to an unprecedented extent.'

The impact of e-business management would be felt primarily in the middle management ranks, Bhattacharyya believed. The conservatism of middle managers has traditionally been the biggest single obstacle to corporate change. But middle management has been indispensable, above all, because it was needed to collect, process and communicate information, the lifeblood of any business. Without accurate data, no business can succeed. Decisions made on the basis of poor data will be poor decisions. 'Three quarters of the problems in business are due to data communication,' said Bhattacharyya. 'Fuzzy information leads to fuzzy actions.'

Alongside accuracy, businesses need speed in data delivery. The leaner and flatter the organisation, the easier it is to capture information quickly. Before the internet, middle managers were essential to collate this material, convert it into accessible form and communicate it. The problem was particularly acute in Britain, because of UK manufacturing industry's relatively low direct-to-indirect labour ratio. Bhattacharyya said, 'Because of the low cost of labour in Britain compared with its advanced competitors, the number of people who worked in a British company was always higher. That was true even after the big redundancies of the early 1980s.'

Awareness of how the internet could change this traditional organisation explained Jack Welch's drive, in the last phase of his career at GE, to convert the whole group to an e-business operational platform. As Welch recognised, the internet delivered transparency and flexibility. It helped a huge combine to move with the nimbleness of an entrepreneurial company. The net made it possible for senior managers to access better data faster, and therefore to take better-informed, quicker decisions – without the large supporting staffs on which they had previously depended.

Bhattacharyya agreed. He forecast that over time, layers of management would be swept away by e-business, and the potential for rapid and radical change would increase exponentially. 'The majority of middle managers are there to manipulate data. With e-business, for the first time, you will crowd out the middle managers. The signal-to-noise ratio in the decision-making process will go up astronomically.'

The internet conferred another big advantage, Bhattacharyya added. For the first time in IT history, it meant that a company that adopted the new generation of information systems did not have to start from scratch after deleting its legacy systems. With the net's vast storage capacity and retrieval capability, data could be retained and recaptured when necessary, in order to inform decision-making going forward.

'Of course, designs are already being made by computers; the enterprise is being managed by computers, supply chain management is done by computers,' Bhattacharyya said. 'The difference now is that you have an information engine that enables you to implement all this without changing the whole scenario: you lose the legacy dimension. That means business transformation will be much faster because you don't need to reinvent things. Fundamentally, for the first time, you are able to use legacy data in all areas, from design management to electronic commerce.'

As a result of the net's ubiquity and accessibility, Bhattacharyya predicted an upsurge in home-working: 'More and more people will be trained to use screens. I expect that, on average, more than 30 per cent of work will be done from home – at a minimum. For the first time, virtual companies will be really virtual.'

The democratic nature of the net created an opportunity for the UK, which despite its improvement thanks to the Thatcher revolution still lagged behind its main rivals, to close the competitiveness gap. 'We have a head-start in the UK, because our schools are developing much more computer-literate people,' Bhattacharyya believed.

However, his international perspective, notably on the developing world, made him acutely aware that the internet created the infrastructure for the most serious threat yet to the primacy of the UK and other developed nations. 'If you look at where the most work is being done on the new information technologies, it is in developing countries such as India. For the first time, your ability to create wealth is not based on whether you are an advanced country or not. By capitalising on the full potential of e-business, a developing nation can leapfrog a so-called advanced economy. So watch out!'

WMG's new Electronic Engineering Business Management programme was being designed, in late 2001, to teach manufacturing industry managers how to operate in the e-age. The content and the ideas that E2 generated, on both the education and the development sides of WMG, would fill the second phase of the International Manufacturing Centre. But not just with manufacturing people.

'The idea is to look at how internet technologies can provide support to manufacturing industries, to collaborate in a virtual environment,' said Raja. 'If you look at any business, be it a manufacturing company or an NHS Trust [WMG was already working with two Trusts in the West Midlands], you always have a procurement process, for example. As soon as you have that and access to the internet, you start asking whether you are doing things the right way or whether, by using e-business, you can improve the operation of the supply chain. So here we are, trying to use the net as a tool to improve procurement.'

E2, Bhattacharyya believed, would have a currency even greater than that enjoyed by his original engineering business management concept. Engineering business management had grown out of his identification of specific British cultural problems: the university–industry divide, and the intra-industry divide between the engineer and the finance man. It was only subsequently that, through its various refinements and extensions, the basic concept had proved applicable internationally. E2, by contrast, was from the outset a global concept developed to meet a global demand. It was universally relevant because the net, Bhattacharyya believed, was the ultimate open system. It posed a challenge to every company, anywhere: 'There is no hiding place any more from the consumer,' he said. 'The slow company and the flabby manager will be exposed as never before.'

Chapter Ten

The Achievement

In May 2000, Gordon Brown, Chancellor of the Exchequer, hailed a breakthrough in the relationship between British universities and British industry. Brown's change agent was a joint venture between Massachusetts Institute of Technology and Cambridge University. Pump-primed by the normally penny-pinching Treasury to the munificent tune of £68m, MIT agreed to establish its first European centre at Cambridge, and the two institutions resolved to develop what both they and Brown proclaimed would be a pioneering venture to promote technological entrepreneurship in the UK.

The MIT–Cambridge link was the product of a classic inward investment battle: Brown had been driven to throw both money and Cambridge at MIT by the prospect that the Americans were about to set up shop in the Republic of Ireland. The effect of the deal, however, was not quite what the Chancellor intended. Among those who tracked the interface between academia and industry in the UK, the move appeared to defy logic. For there could be no doubt which British organisation was the natural partner of MIT, and it was not resident in Silicon Fen.

From his office at WMG, Bhattacharyya watched the publicity hoopla surrounding the MIT–Cambridge link-up with a mixture of disappointment and amusement. Disappointment because he knew that MIT's closest soul-mate in the British academic world was Warwick. Their past connections proved that, as did their philosophy. But Bhattacharyya, a positive thinker *sans pareil*, did not dwell on that disappointment for long. Instead, he was amused by the irony that underlay the MIT–Cambridge deal. This was, in effect, an extraordinary act of government intervention. The Treasury was importing, at considerable cost, a giant American group to provide the kind of expertise in academia–industry collaboration that had already been developed by a small and successful British group.

The Treasury action may have been crass, but it also paid Bhattacharyya an inadvertent and supreme compliment. The truth was that, two decades and many thousands of customers on, WMG still stood head and shoulders above other British universities in the effectiveness of its approach to industry. 'Other people come to us and talk about working with us, but Kumar Bhattacharyya is different,' said Rob Meakin, Marconi's human resources director, in July 2001. 'Unlike the others, he really understands what companies need. And in order to deliver what they need, he is always prepared to go out on a limb for his customers.'

Meakin, at the time deeply involved in the effort to turn round the stricken telecoms group, had good reason to appreciate Bhattacharyya's commitment. But by the time he offered that laudation, WMG had garnered a raft of plaudits from both companies and countries. As early as 1993, the French government had sent a study team to examine Warwick's modus operandi. Its report concluded: 'This is Europe's most outstanding example of how a university should interact with industry.' Four years later, the German government followed suit. 'Warwick Manufacturing

Group is a future role model for German universities,' a government report said. In the same year, Singapore's economic development board recommended that: 'Singapore should look at the WMG and clone it.'

Yet in Britain, Bhattacharyya was something of a prophet without honour. Meakin recalled being asked in early 2001 by the vice-chancellor of one university that was trying to get closer to industry: 'We know a bit about Bhattacharyya, but what exactly is it that Warwick does?' In November 2000, when University College, London, announced it was establishing a postgraduate research centre on a technology park in East Anglia in alliance with British Telecommunications, to try to build links with industry, a BT executive commented: 'We believe this is the first time that a university faculty has gone to industry.'

Like Brown's patronage of the MIT–Cambridge connection, such ignorance of WMG's work cut two ways. On one side, it emphasised Bhattacharyya's continuing pre-eminence. Barry Cohen of PTC, Warwick's long-standing Cad/Cam partner, said: 'Warwick has a very unique history. Its commitment to providing teaming and innovation created a new paradigm for manufacturing strategy, particularly in Europe, that allowed WMG to emerge with a new niche. They were the first to recognise that innovation is a function not only of logic, but of process and people; that competitiveness is not only a matter of new technology, but of leadership in defining new processes.'

Cohen also recognised Bhattacharyya's marketing flair and his grasp of the big picture: 'He is always on the look-out for ways to put together a showcase that demonstrates full capability. He sees pieces of the equation and fits them into a package that demonstrates what's possible. And because of his background, he understood about globalisation. All of that makes Warwick a very special forum: the people there are leading industry, they are thinking about social and economic policy and how it relates to business and technology. You can have conversations there across industry that you can't have anywhere else. That is all part of the Warwick experience.'

Yet from the perspective of UK plc, Bhattacharyya's continued isolation at the cutting edge of the industry–academia partnership was less than splendid. It is hard to escape this conclusion: that the two principal competitive weaknesses that British industry carried into the twenty-first century – lack of quality management and lack of a robust technological base – were related to the failure of others, on both sides of the historic divide, to understand and emulate the Warwick model.

Evincing a degree of humility that would surprise his critics, Bhattacharyya does not put it quite like that. He makes no bones about British industry's fundamental flaw – 'too much short-term profit, not enough long-term product' – but attributes it partly to the history's legacy. 'To have a technologically capable manufacturing sector, you need a technology base. The fact is that twenty years ago, with a few exceptions, we were bankrupt of technology and manufacturing industry was starved of quality people. The government drove everything.'

Britain has raised its game in the ensuing two decades, but its rivals have not stood still. 'We aren't a bad manufacturing nation,' says Bhattacharyya. 'Foreign companies have invested here and done well. But we have four big problems. We don't have a base big enough for any product to succeed in the home market alone. Partly as a result of this, a large majority of companies here don't have a product base because they have never invested consistently in R&D. We have also forgotten that, even if you have a good product at the conceptual stage, you need attention to detail to make it a commercial proposition. Finally, you need a national policy framework that helps products to be made successfully. Our policies have improved, but it's too late for many companies. They have lost too much ground. The world has globalised and they have got an uphill struggle.'

Yet the rigorous analyst in Bhattacharyya sits beside the

passionate forward thinker and the committed teacher. The pioneer believes Britain's economic recovery can be sustained. The teacher sees enormous promise in the IT literacy of the current school generation. As usual with Bhattacharyya, that hope is not the product of pie-in-the-sky blind faith, but grounded in grassroots reality. From his earliest days at Warwick, Bhattacharyya kept in close touch with local schools. On a visit to Warwick after being appointed Secretary of State for Education in the second Blair government, Estelle Morris recalled her first visit to the University, when she was a Coventry secondary school-teacher in the 1980s. Bhattacharyya had invited a number of teachers from the City to discuss the education of children for working life. 'I will never forget that meeting,' Morris said. 'It was the first time that I, as a teacher, had ever been asked my opinion on these vital issues.'

To convert that potential into individual and national prosperity, Bhattacharyya says Britain must do one thing above all others. 'What we require is a framework that encourages entrepreneurs. You can teach people how to exploit their innate ability; you can make sure that technology is exploited. The connecting factor is entrepreneurialism. Entrepreneurs have to be supported with processes. But if you have that base, then you can create a framework for entrepreneurs to succeed.'

That view is driven by self-recognition. 'How can an Indian come here and break all the rules in a very traditional environment?' The question is rhetorical. 'Even today, people come and look and go back completely surprised that we have actually done it. I'm lucky. I'm not a manager; I have some good administrators who clear up the mess that I create. But I am also surrounded by a lot of people who are prepared to try the apparently impossible, people with whom I can brainstorm. To build our client relationships, we have two basic rules: we are completely transparent and we take calculated risks.'

Those are not the kind of rules that you will find in a manual, because Bhattacharyya wrote his own textbook. Alan Curtis has known him as long as anyone and longer than most: 'He has pioneered ways of working closely with companies. He has disregarded the traditional university system. That has landed him in all sorts of trouble, but because of his success, he has been allowed to operate a profit centre in the middle of the university. That has given him freedom to a degree that other people in similar environments can't contemplate. He will invest money up-front without immediate return. He has never waited for a contract. If he feels it's the right thing to do, he will do it. From the earliest days, he has gone out with that judgement.'

Those are hallmarks of the classic entrepreneur. What made Bhattacharyya special was the application of those qualities to the environment in which he operated, and the space that he found and filled. Those who doubt his distinctive achievement might recall a latin phrase: *Sic Monumentum Requiris, Circumspice* – If you need a monument, look around.

You should look in both directions on which Bhattacharyya has himself focused. In the academic world outside America, there are many outstanding management education insitutions, but none that focusses so completely and effectively on the interface between university, design engineering centre and manufacturing process. So robust – to borrow a phrase – is the Bhattacharyya model that it has proved capable of multiplication into all fields of engineering and of extrapolation into the service sector. Today, WMG executives are at work in the most inhospitable zone confronting British managers – the National Health Service. They are helping a group of Birmingham hospitals to improve their management processes, notably their supply chain skills. Bhattacharyya has never been someone who ducked a challenge, no matter how formidable.

Look, too, at the area of his first and greatest challenge – the attempt to transform the quality of British manufacturing management. On the face of it, this effort has met with only mixed success. Since the eighties, the competitiveness of British management has undoubtedly been transformed. Yet, during the same period, the term 'British' manufacturing has become redundant in numerous sectors. Many engineering companies have been gobbled up by predators from overseas. Whole industries, such as vehicle-making, have passed into foreign ownership.

But in many, if not most, cases, those operations live on in Britain, despite the foreign ownership, despite the level of the pound. Take Bhattacharyya's original client, BL. The future of Longbridge under MG Rover seemed problematic, but Cowley, rechristened Oxford, is busy turning out BMW's highly successful MINI range. At Solihull, Land Rover under Ford's ownership has the potential for long-term growth. Bhattacharyya's contribution to equipping these and many other operations for survival, or even prosperity, in the 21st century should not be underestimated. Without the eyes and minds that were opened by Warwick's engineering business management, the future would have been bleaker, or non-existent.

Bhattacharyya has also been a front-line soldier in a bigger battle, the battle for manufacturing industry itself. Despite the obvious fact that America's economic recovery was powered by the resurgence of its manufacturing industry against Japanese competition, Britain has been dogged for much of the past two decades with primitive theories about the post-industrial society, the knowledge-based society – as if that rendered manufacturing itself obsolete.

Today, the battle to recognise the importance of manufacturing-related activity has been won, in most hearts and minds at least. Assembly may take place offshore, but the manufacturing chain – in its modern, holistic sense of product conception and design to marketing and selling – is recognised as an essential engine of economic growth. 'No single group can change what has happened, but at least we have helped to bring respectability to manufacturing,' Bhattacharyya said in early 2002. 'It is not perceived to be metal-bashing any more. In the UK, manufacturing industry was brought into high focus with government because of us.' Indeed, the DTI's innovation unit was created during Peter Lilley's tenure on the initiative of Bhattacharyya. 'Years and years of neglect can't be changed overnight, but what's important is that there are people who have been educated with us and who are now working in many industries in the UK,' he said. 'What would have happened if we had not been there? Those managers would not have the skills they are deploying today.'

Overseas, Bhattacharyya faced no such prejudices and preconceptions. He merely had to establish WMG as a world-renowned institution. In that, too, he succeeded: 'We were for a long time, and still are in many senses, *the* academic centre for manufacturing industry.' Today, his creation stands alone – except for the appreciation of several prime ministers, a few presidents and about 5,000 coporate customers worldwide.

Select Bibliography

Barnett, C., *The Audit of War*, Macmillan, 1986.

Hoskyns, J., *Just In Time*, Aurum Press, 2000.

Lorenz, A., *A Fighting Chance*, Hutchinson, 1989.

Newhouse, J., *The Sporty Game*, Alfred A Knopf 1982.

Owen, G., *From Empire to Europe*, HarperCollins 1999.

Wiener, M.J., *English Culture and the Decline of the Industrial Spirit*, Cambridge University Press 1981.

The Sunday Times: various articles 1989–2001.

Warwick Manufacturing Group: speeches, papers and publications 1980–2002.

Index

108, 111, 118
Day, Sir Graham, 32, 35, 37
demonstrator projects, 88, 89
Department of Trade and
 Industry
 industrial competitiveness,
  encouragement of, 99
 and Rover takeover by BMW,
  60–61
Deutschmark, 126–127
'Developing You' (BAE/WMG
 education programme),
 76–77
Donohue, Martin, 98, 102, 104
Durban Westville University,
 150–151

e-business, 111, 182–184,
 197–198
 significance of, 198–201
 and technology management
  programme (Marconi/
  WMG), 176, 177
 Westbury, 114, 115–116, 117
 see also internet
E2 (electronic engineering
 business management), 182,
 183, 197–198, 201
Eco-Tek, 46
electricity supply industry, South
 Africa (Eskom), 142–144
engine development, 36, 40
 aerospace industry, 66–67,
  68–69

car industry, 32–35, 36, 40
engineering
 concurrent, 193–194
 education/training, 8–9, 13,
  14
 financial training, importance
  of, 14, 26
 modelling, 191
 reverse, 191
 status of, 13–14, 15
engineering data management
 (EDM), 189, 190, 194–195
Engineering Our Future, 8–9
*English Culture and the Decline of
 the Industrial Spirit*, 10–11
Enterprise Resource Planning
 (ERP), 189, 190
entrepreneurs, importance of,
 207
Escort (Ford), 36
Eskom, 142–144, 146, 147,
 155–156, 157
European Aeronautic, Defence
 and Space (EADS)
 company, 95
Evans, Dick (later Sir Richard),
 74, 80
Exchange Rate Mechanism
 (ERM), 126
exchange rates, 126–127

Federal Drug Administration
 (US), 128–129
Ferrie, John, 56, 66, 69–71

WMG), 164

Lean Aerospace Initiative (LAI), 91

lean manufacturing, 7, 16–17, 91–92, 102

  BAE Systems, introduction at, 75–76, 92, 93

  Rover, introduction at, 38, 39, 40

Lean Wing partnership, 85–93, 95–96

learning agreements (BAE/ WMG), 78

Leyland Cars, 25, 26

Lib-Lab Pact, 7

Lilley, Peter, 209–210

London Electricity, 44

Longbridge (Rover plant), 39, 40, 209

Losec, 133

Lucas, 6–7, 9

Lucent, 180

Lycos, 173

Lygo, Admiral Sir Raymond, 73

Machine That Changed the World, The, 102

Maestro (Austin Rover), 22, 29, 33

Mahathir Mohamad, 48

Major, John, 61–62

Malaysia, 48–49

Malaysian Industry Group for Higher Technology

(MIGHT), 49

management education

  Bhattacharyya's philosophy of, 15–16

  need for, 13

  1990's recession, effect of, 54–56

  'traditional' approach, 16

  see also Warwick Manufacturing Group (WMG)

manufacturing industry

  current state, 209–210

  and overseas companies, 65, 209

  problems, 206

  status of, 14–15, 209

  technology, significance of, 17, 18, 206

Marconi *see* GEC (General Electric Company)/ Marconi

Marconi Electronic Systems, 80–83

  sale by GEC (General Electric Company), 79–80, 161–163, 166–167, 169

Marconi SpA, 166, 169

Marcus, Roy, 139, 140, 141, 151

market pull manufacturing, 16–17

Marshall's, 107

Massachusetts Institute of

pound, strength of, 126–127
PowerGen, 144
prefabrication, housebuilding
    sector, 103, 106, 107–109
Prilosec, 133
Process Business Management
    (PBM), 125, 127
process industries
    educational programmes, lack
        of, 124
    manufacturing, importance of,
        130
    and Warwick Manufacturing
        Group (WMG), 125–126,
        127–128, 131
procurement programme (BAE/
    WMG), 77
Project 2000 (South Africa),
    148–149
Proton, 49
Puttick, John, 123, 129–130

Raja, Vinesh, 187–188, 188
Ramashala, Mapule, 151
RB211 engine, Rolls-Royce, 67,
    68
recession
    early 1990's, 54
    late 1970's/early 1980's,
        20–21
Reitzle, Wolfgang, 59
Reltec, 170
reverse-engineering, 191
Reynolds, Clive, 38, 56, 125,

172
Rhys, Garel, 58
Robins, Sir Ralph, 67, 68
Roche, 119–120, 121
Rolls-Royce, 22, 32, 56
    RB211 engine, 67, 68
    Trent engine, 67–69
Rover, 26, 32, 33, 35, 186
    BMW takeover, 59–61, 74
    Phoenix consortium takeover
        (2000), 58
    production methods, reform,
        37–40
    simulation techniques, use of,
        28
    and Warwick Manufacturing
        Group (WMG), 37–40,
        163–165, 186
Roy, Rajat, 21–22, 28, 98–99
    see also Westbury, and
        Warwick Manufacturing
        Group (WMG)
Royal Ordnance, 73
Royal Society, 140
Ruffels, Phil, 66, 68, 69

Safea (State Administration for
    Foreign Export Affairs),
    51–52
Schmidt, Steve, 177
school leavers, lack of science/
    maths students, 180
schools, and information
    technology, 196–197, 207

science, attitudes towards, 14–15
Semcoe (Sun European
    Manufacturing Centre of
    Excellence), 184, 189–192
Shacklock, Tim, 74
Siemens, 166
Simoes, Fernando, 138
Simpson, George (later Lord),
    37, 79, 80, 163, 166–167,
    181
simulation techniques, 28,
    29–30, 34
simultaneous engineering,
    193–194
Smit, Ben, 159
Smith, Gordon, 33
Smith, Professor Sir Roland, 73,
    74
Snow, C P, 14
Society of British Aerospace
    Companies (SBAC), 91, 92
Society of Motor Manufacturers
    and Traders (SMMT), 91,
    99–100
Software in Schools initiative,
    196–197
South Africa
    affirmative action policy, 143
    economic development
        strategy, 148–150,
        158–160
    electricity supply industry/
        Eskom, 142–144,
        155–156, 157

KwaZulu–Natal, 151–152,
    155
liberalisation, 139
management education, need
    for, 139, 148, 149, 153
MBA courses, 'dumping',
    141–142
Northern Province, 152–155
privatisations, 148, 159
protectionist policies, effects
    of, 139, 149
regional development,
    149–150
science/technology
    development, 140, 149
universities, 150–151
and Warwick Manufacturing
    Group (WMG), 139–141,
    142, 144–148, 149–153,
    154–159, 160
women, management
    education, 156–157
Space4, 107–108, 115
Stairways, 112
Statistical Process Control (SPC),
    88–89
steel industry, national strike
    (1979–80), 27
sterling, strength of, 126–127
Storey, Dr. David, 12
Sun Microsystems, 184,
    186–187, 188–189
    see also Semcoe (Sun European
        Manufacturing Centre of